iTeachMe

iTeachMe

Maximizing Student Comprehension

Dingane Baruti M.D., FAAFP

Andrea McMiller MPA

Mariah Olivia Dean

iTeachMe

Copyright© 2011 by Dingane Baruti MD. All rights reserved. Printed in the United States of America. Except as permitted under the United States Copyright Act of 1976, no part of this publication may be reproduced in any form or by any means, or stored in a database or retrieval system, without the prior, written permission of the publisher.

Cover design by Jennifer Bischoff

ISBN-10: 0-983-4221-1-7
ISBN-13: 978-0-9834221-1-2

Library of Congress Control Number: **2011907611**

Cataloging-in-Publication Data

Baruti, D.
    iTeachMe: Maximizing Student Comprehension / D. Baruti
p. cm.
    Includes index.
    ISBN 0-983-4221-1-7 (paper)
      1. Education. 2. Self-Improvement 3. Study Skills 4. Success

Banneker-DuBois Publishing   Banneker-DuBois Publishing

Atlanta

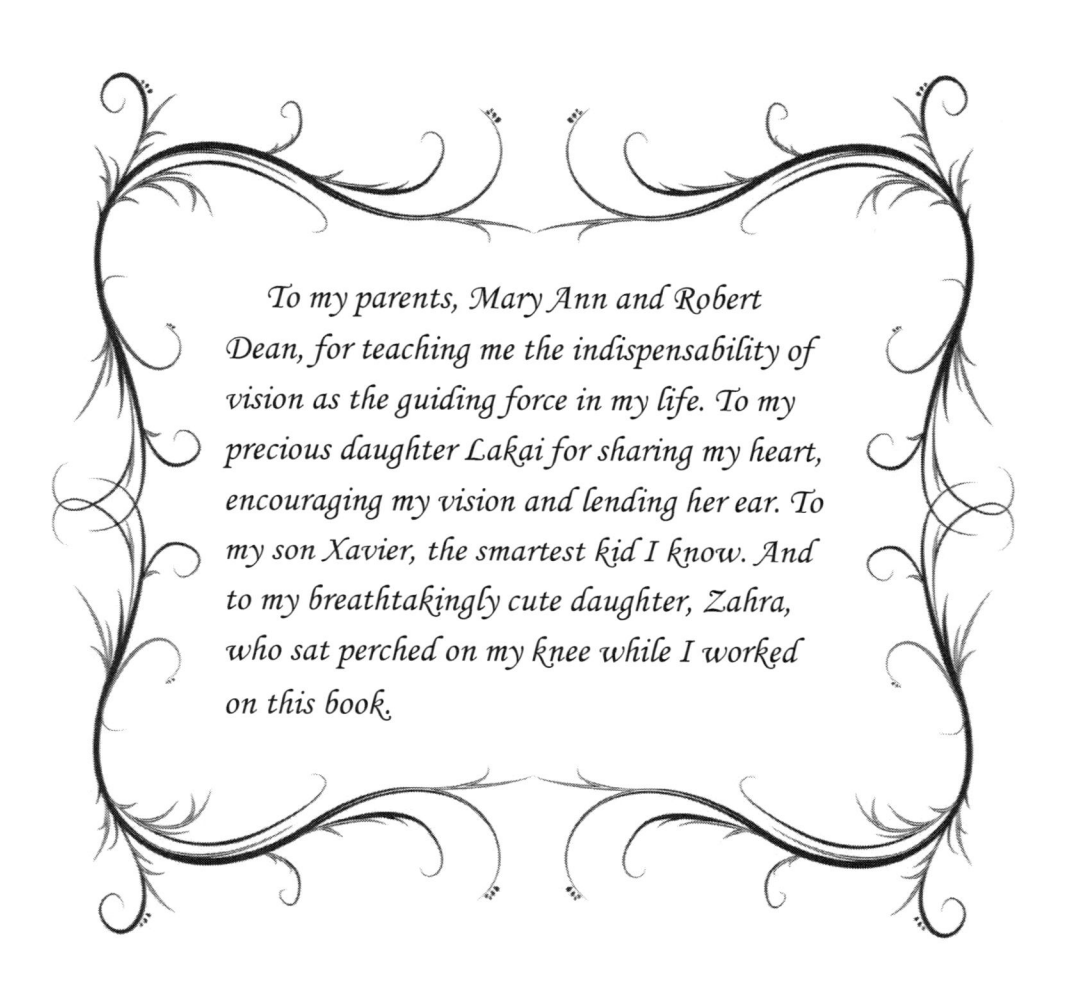

To my parents, Mary Ann and Robert Dean, for teaching me the indispensability of vision as the guiding force in my life. To my precious daughter Lakai for sharing my heart, encouraging my vision and lending her ear. To my son Xavier, the smartest kid I know. And to my breathtakingly cute daughter, Zahra, who sat perched on my knee while I worked on this book.

Contents

Preface 7

Introduction 13

1. **Life Atmosphere** 18

2. **How We Learn** 36

3. **And the Band Played On** 47

4. **The Sacred Self** 67

5. **How to Do iTeachMe** 84

Step-by-Step iTeachMe Instructions 86

Appendix A: iTeachMe Preparation 99

Appendix B: iTeachMe Steps 100

Appendix C: Germany's *Lernen durch Lehren* 102

Appendix D: Author Biography 105

Bibliography 112

Preface

iTeachMe: Maximizing Student Comprehension was written as a collaborative effort by Andrea McMiller; high school student, Mariah Olivia Dean and myself. We kept this book to approximately 100 pages so that high school and college students could read it in one sitting. We conscientiously avoid superfluous information as we introduce a new home study method called the iTeachMe method that literally guarantees straight A's. Although this book was written for high school students and up, teachers, school administrators and education policy makers will also find the information we present useful.

I did not discover the iTeachMe method. It was introduced to me by the most upright and morally solid man that I have ever known, my dad, Robert G. Dean. It was July of 1992; I had just returned home to Bakersfield, California from a 2 1/2 year stint in the US Army. When my father saw how bright-eyed and bushy-tailed I was about starting school at the local junior college, he promptly gave me an old, thin, tattered book with the pages falling out. The once glossy-white front cover had dulled to an off-white color. The book could not have been more than 65 pages front to back. The title --- *The Overnight Student*: *How I Went From Straight F's To Straight A's*, by Dr. Michael L. Jones. The book was basically a protracted testimonial of how Dr. Jones successfully turned his poor academic performance around by applying a study method taken directly from the Bible.

What was the study method --- learn-by-teach. Dr. Jones extracted this learning theory from the first five books of the Old Testament, the Pentateuch. In the Mosaic Law, the people of Israel were commanded to teach the Law to their children several times a day. Even for experienced Theology students, understanding the Mosaic Law with all its nuances and foreshadowing is no walk in the park. Jones surmised that toddlers would not have had the cognitive capacity to understand even the simplest aspects of the Law. So why should their parents teach it to them? Jones concluded that this divine command was given, not to benefit the children as much as it was to benefit the parents. Jones' conclusion was as profound as it was simple. The God of Abraham, Isaac and Jacob; Elohim; the Most High; Yahweh himself has a preferred method for placing His Law into his children's hearts --- make them teach it.

Dr. Jones did not give this divine Learn-by-teach method any particular name, but other historical figures did. The Socratic Method is closely related to this biblical method. Throughout human history, brilliant men and women continue to discover and rediscover the superiority of the Learn-by-teach method over all other learning techniques. The *Epistulae morales ad Lucilium* is a collection of letters written in 4 BCE to Lucilius, the Governor of Sicily by the prominent Roman philosopher, Seneca. In one of his letters, Seneca wrote *docendo discimus*. Just in case your Latin is a bit rusty, *docendo discmus* means, *by teaching we are learning*.

To teach is to attach meaning to knowledge and then present this meaningful knowledge to someone else in a logical, coherent fashion. There is one word that describes this whole meaning-to-knowledge cognitive process --- <u>understanding</u>. This is why that of everything there is to get in life, an understanding is second to none. Why do students in mainland China perform so well on math and science exams? While the students may appear to be passive learners while in the classroom, when they are at home, many of them strive to attach meaning to the knowledge they received in school that day (Xu, 2007). So, when they are tested, they produce answers from a genuine understanding of the material, and not from mere recognition of the correct multiple-choice answer.

The vast majority of American students do not use learn-by-teach study methods. Despite our brightest education researchers urging us to adopt learn-by-teach methods, American students are still taught by the traditional authoritative teaching model. In the US, educational policies are not established by best practices or by evidence-based research. Our educational policies are established by various social and religious groups who use their political and economic power to inject their own world views into school curricula at the local and state levels. So while students in other countries fully engage higher math, advanced chemistry and quantum physics, American students remain stagnant, unwitting pawns in a national chess game between liberals and conservatives. It is no wonder that in 2006, US high school students placed 29th of 57 in science and 35th of 57 in math (Organization for Economic Co-operation & Development OCED).

But just because the United States has not used learn-by-teach methods in the past, does not mean that we cannot adopt this method now. After all, this transition occurred in Germany in the early 80's when German professor Jean-Pol Martin discovered his own learn-by-teach method. He called his method *Lernen durch Lehren (LdL)*, which, of course, means Learn-by-teach. So successful was Professor Martin's *Lernen durch Lehren* method in improving the academic performance of German students, that the

German federal government adopted and disseminated the method to post-secondary institutions throughout all of Germany. Why can't this happen in the United States? After all, we do have our own learn-by-teach method; it is called iTeachMe. Because the iTeachMe method does not require a classroom audience, it lends itself particularly well to solo use at home. This is why I believe that the American iTeachMe method is an improvement over Germany's classroom-based *Lernen durch Lehren* method.

The iTeachMe method is not some closely guarded secret for the academic elite, like aspiring physicians, engineers, or rocket scientists. This method is actually such an easy and natural way to learn that serious students accidentally stumble upon it in their quest to improve their understanding in a broad range of disciplines. This is precisely the reason why I asked Mrs. Andrea McMiller to write the first part of chapter one. Unlike me, Mrs. McMiller did not find the iTeachMe method by having someone give it to her. She discovered it on her own when the circumstances of her early childhood compelled her to pretend that she was an elementary school teacher. Andrea was an intensely shy little girl. At home in rural Eastern Alabama, her childhood home life was not conducive to, and did not facilitate a secular education. She never quite fit in with her classmates and reports being ridiculed by them throughout much of her elementary school years. Andrea coped with her loneliness by engaging in role play. At home, she would pretend to be the teacher and taught her homework lessons to herself while standing in the mirror.

Pretending to be the teacher, Andrea was able to step outside of her little-shy-girl identity and into a more powerful social role of teacher, someone immune to ridicule of mere children. Andrea used her own homework assignments as her teaching material at home. Little did this six year old girl know that she was doing the very same learn-by-teach method that Socrates, Plato, Aristotle, Seneca, the Old Testament Jews, John Dewey, and Professor Jean Pol Martin used. Young children are generally protected and valued by societies because of the enormous potential they have for the continued existence and advancement of that society. But as a child, Andrea was not thus protected or valued. Once you read more about her difficult childhood, you will see that from the very beginning of her life, the cards were ominously stacked against her. Instead of being the most likely to succeed, she was actually the most likely to fail, at least academically. But she did not fail; she excelled. She excelled simply because she stumbled onto an ancient method for genuinely educating herself, the iTeachMe method.

The iTeachMe method works for students from high school and up. To demonstrate the iTeachMe method's effectiveness for high school students, I asked my 16 year old, accomplished niece, Mariah Olivia Dean to write the first part of chapter five. Mariah is a junior at Benjamin E. Mays High School in Atlanta, Georgia. She has been using the iTeachMe study method ever since she was a freshman. When people meet Mariah they quickly find out why I call her accomplished. When she was 11, she was attacked by a dog and had the front muscle group of her right leg bitten off. She received the best reconstructive surgical care at Stanford University Medical Center in California. With 14 months of physical therapy and dogged perseverance she learned to walk again, and without any assistive devices. But for Mariah, it was not enough that she simply walked again. In junior high school, she went out for the basketball team. Although she walked with a limp, she made the team, out-competed her competitors through sheer determination and became an asset to her team.

Two years later when she started high school, she was not discouraged by the higher level of competition and went out for the basketball team there too. Fast forward two and a half years to today. She is the starting center and captain of the varsity team and quite a fierce competitor. She remains active in her local church and is on the Advanced Placement track. Despite her busy extra-curricular schedule and A.P. classes, she maintains a 3.9 G.P.A and averages 16 points, 8 blocks and 7 rebounds per game. On a recent AP Biology laboratory exam where everyone in the class scored less than 65%, Mariah answered every question correctly, plus earned extra points, for a score 102%. Mariah's teacher asked her how she was able to get such a high score when the class average score was so low. Mariah quickly answered --- iTeachMe.

Andrea's and Mariah's experience with the iTeachMe method can be found at the beginning of chapters one and five, respectively. The behavioral, psychological and neuro-biological aspects of the iTeachMe method are presented by me, after 19 years of applying the iTeachMe principles various classes and teaching it to college and medical students from California to Maryland. Any grammatical errors, misspellings or poorly written parts are completely my fault. Students who read this book have already taken the first step toward using the iTeachMe method. This book, specifically chapter five, serves as the instruction manual for applying the ancient study method at home. All of the other materials that you will need to perform iTeachMe at home, the 37 inch x 48 inch, laminated iTeachMe Wall Lecture Chart, a two-tiered adjustable-height lectern, an iTeachMe Recursive Review Planner, can be purchased from the iTeachMe Company at www.iteachme.net.

DB

Introduction

As Americans we tend to believe that we are exceptional in most everything we do. Many of us would like to think that we are more advanced than other countries in many aspects of social living. Although the appropriateness of this belief is quite arguable today, it certainly could have rung true at some earlier point in our country's history. In the past few decades numerous country-comparison surveys clearly show that the United States lags behind other less developed countries in the quality of compulsory education. In 2000, an intergovernmental agency of 57 member countries called the Organization for Economic Cooperation and Development developed a survey that compares the academic performance of students across international lines. This international academic comparison survey is called PISA, which is short for *Program for International Student Assessment*. In 2006, all fifty-seven countries, including the United States participated in PISA. On this survey, American teenagers scored below average in science literacy and math (Organization for Economic Co-operation & Development OCED).

The 2006 PISA report also included a summary of earlier retrospective surveys that compared the academic performance of students within individual countries over time. The summarized report showed that from 1963 to 1980, American high school students' SAT scores dropped more than 50 points in the critical reading section and nearly 40 points in the math section. The summarized report also found that 40% of the 17-year-old American students tested could not draw inferences from written material. Sixty-six percent of them could not solve simple math problems that required several steps. A staggering 80% could not write a persuasive essay.

These disheartening findings are consistent with the results of President Reagan's 1983 National Commission on Excellence in Education (NCEE). This commission was headed up by then Secretary of Education T.H. Bell who was tasked to assess the quality of education at the primary, secondary and postsecondary levels in public and private schools. The commission also compared American high schools and colleges with those of other economically developed nations. The final report, primarily written by James J. Harvey, concluded that while the United States at one time was the unchallenged world leader in commerce, industry and science that as of 1983 "the educational foundations of our society are presently being eroded by a rising tide of mediocrity that threatens our very future as a nation" (NCEE, 1983). So moved by the looming threat of our country's eroding educational system, Harvey further penned that "if an unfriendly foreign power had attempted to impose on America the mediocre educational performance that exists today, we might well have viewed it as an act of war" (NCEE, 1983).

But the US is not the only country with a deteriorating educational system. Both Finland and South Korea faced similar education woes that the US now faces. But the good news for them and the hopeful news for the US is that both Finland and South Korea turned their failing educational systems around. For example,

Starting in the 1980s, for example, Finland dismantled the rigid tracking system that had allocated differential access to knowledge to its young people and eliminated the state-mandated testing system that was used for this purpose, replacing them with highly trained teachers educated in newly overhauled schools of education, along with curriculums and assessments focused on problem-solving, creativity and independent learning. These changes have propelled achievement to the top of the international rankings and closed what was once a large, intractable achievement gap.

In the space of one generation, South Korea has transformed itself from a nation that educated less than a quarter of its citizens through high school to one that graduates more than 95 percent from high school and ranks third in college-educated adults, with most young people now completing postsecondary education. Egalitarian access to schools and a common curriculum, coupled with investments in well-prepared teachers, have been part of the national strategy there as well (Darling-Hammond, 2010).

As of 2011, the United States has not gotten the message that Finland and South Korea got more than thirty years ago. As our country rushes headlong toward our own perception of superior technology, we use progressively less of our individual cognitive skills and reasoning abilities. Yes! Our gee-whiz iPads and amazing smart phones are making it less necessary for us to actually think, calculate and reason. The embarrassing irony here is that we do not even know how to repair our superior technological devices when they malfunction. We rely on the technologically savvy youngsters in India to repair our computers and smart phones. This cognitive laziness puts a serious drag on American intellectual development. Throughout all of human civilization, successive generations have become more intellectually developed than previous ones. But the US is the only Western nation that seems to be regressing intellectually. Just consider what it meant to be educated or of the learned gentry 2,300 years ago. Great thinkers like Socrates, Plato and Aristotle spent their entire lives exercising their reasoning and analytical skills. Just consider the true story of a little boy named Alex.

Alex was born to royalty in Macedonia in year 356 BCE. Desiring a formal education for their toddler son, King Philip II of Macedonia and his wife Queen Olympias hired tutors to educate the lad. Leonidis was Alex's first tutor and taught the boy math, archery and horsemanship. Then Lysimachus started tutoring the boy and devised an interactive, role-play game for Alex to play. During this game, Alex impersonated Achilles, the fabled, mighty warrior of Homer's *Iliad*. When Alex turned 13, his father asked the great philosopher Aristotle to tutor his son. For three years, Aristotle taught Alex philosophy, government, politics, poetry, drama and science.

Alex's military career began very early at age 16. Of course, just like any other teenager, he had difficulties transitioning from childhood to adulthood. When he turned 20, Alex's father was assassinated, making Alex King of Macedonia. To secure his position as king, Alexander ruled with an iron hand, eventually gaining control of the larger part of Greece. Once he controlled the majority of Greece, he was well-positioned to, and eventually did conquer both the Persian and Egyptian empires. Alexander the Great's early education gave him the tools to conquer the known world. While he may have been a ruthless military general and monarch, he was also quite thoroughly educated. Now compare Alexander's education and exploits as a teenager to contemporary American high school students. Today, even our top-performing high school seniors, with all of their technological gadgets could hardly match wits with Alexander. Just ask today's graduating high school valedictorians to talk intelligently about current U.S.

politics. Ask them to describe the goings on in our country from 1861 to 1865. Ask them to point out China on an unlabeled map.

In order to reverse the erosion of American intellectualism, our students must return to the ancient methods of educating themselves --- learning by teaching. An education can never be given; it must always be taken. Ancient study methods like the Socratic Method or the Elenchus Method fully engaged students' reasoning powers and required them to integrate new concepts into their existing knowledge base. The students were then required to demonstrate this cognitive integration by talking, asking questions or teaching the new concept to others. After German university professors re-discovered their own version of the Socratic Method, the LdL, they disseminated it nationally then introduced it to universities in both Japan and Russia. Except for St. John's University in Annapolis, Maryland, no American university consistently uses the LdL method or any other learn-by-teach method.

iTeachMe: Maximizing Student Comprehension seeks to change this reality by introducing the ancient learn-by-teach study method to American living rooms, high schools and colleges. The iTeachMe home study method can be viewed as the American version of Germany's LdL--- but only with improvements. The iTeachMe method helps students transfer newly learned concepts from their short-term to their long-term memories by using four techniques: (1) **rapid input**, (2) **cognitive integration**, (3) **active output** and (4) **recursive review**. If our students begin using these techniques, the least they would do is earn straight A's. But the most they would do is educate the core of their selves and propel the US to the forefront of intellectual leadership for the 21st century.

Chapter 1
Life Atmosphere

Before we discuss education and specific studying techniques, we must first put compulsory education in its proper context. By compulsory, I mean the mandatory education that is required for all American youth, grades K – 12. It is useful for us to consider the practical role of education in our lives. Why do we need to take an education? What genuine benefits do educated people have over uneducated or poorly educated ones? Just like Alexander the Great took a formal education during the first two decades of his life, many societies throughout history tend to concentrate formal education activities into the first 20 years of their youngsters' lives.

Children are generally more impressionable than adults and are more apt to learn new concepts, languages and technological skills. But this enhanced aptitude does not automatically produce educated adults. The journey to an educated adult heart takes a great deal of intrinsic drive. A person's life circumstance may either augment or inhibit this drive. Life is time. And time is just a collection of moments or seconds. Seconds, minutes, hours and days, we have approximately 25 thousand days to live and to contribute to humankind's collective experience. Time is priceless. It is far more valuable than either wealth or health. The wealthiest person and the healthiest person on earth both need time to enjoy their wealth and their health. Once time has passed it can never be recovered again. How we use our 25 thousand days is largely determined by our life atmospheres. One's life atmosphere is determined by the complex interaction of birthplace, birth era, family, religion and socioeconomic class. We certainly do not choose our life atmospheres; we are merely born into them. The prevailing tone of a person's life may be loud, cluttered and busy. On the other hand, a person's life tone may be peaceful, simple and goal-directed.

Although we cannot control our life atmospheres, we can control our behavior within them. A child born during Germany's Third Reich does not have to be anti-Semitic as an adult. Black children born under the scourge of colonial American slavery do not have to horsewhip their own children like slaves. A person born to illiterate parents does not have to be an illiterate adult. Although we have the ability to determine the course of our lives, fighting against the reality of our life atmosphere is no easy task. It would be very difficult for a person born into Germany's Third Reich to treat Jewish people with respect. Not impossible, but certainly difficult. It would be difficult for an 18th century South Carolinian slave to discipline her school aged son without physically striking him. It would also be difficult for a person born into a family that does not value education to take an education. Of these three examples, perhaps the taking of an education is the more difficult task. Taking an education requires a lifetime of sustained effort; it requires people to cultivate specific habits that store meaningful knowledge deep within the core of their hearts.

Life Atmosphere's Effect on Education

Alexander the Great was born into privilege. Although history teaches us that his parents, King Philip II and his mother Queen Olympias were not too fond of each other, both parents were heavily invested in their son's education. Taking an education was probably easy for Alex. His privileged life atmosphere most likely facilitated his taking of a world-class education. Yes, his education was likely a world-class one. After all, the Great Aristotle was the boy's personal tutor for three years. But consider a historical figure less famous than Alexander the Great and without a world-class education --- Epictetus.

Epictetus was born a slave 55 years after the crucifixion of Jesus Christ. He was born in the city of Hierapolis, what is now considered modern-day Turkey. In his youth Epictetus was enslaved to a master who was insanely jealous of the slave's unquenchable thirst for knowledge. Epictetus took an education by surreptitiously teaching himself philosophy. As he became more proficient in philosophical thought, his master took notice and tried to quell the slave's thirst for knowledge by having his leg broken. It is not known how Epictetus gained his freedom, but he eventually did and began teaching philosophy in Rome at age 38. So moving was his public discourse that Epictetus became widely sought after by dignitaries and heads of state the world over.

Unlike Alexander the Great, Epictetus did not conquer a single individual. He did not wage war or set up governments. But just like Alexander, Epictetus educated the core of himself. Not only did the ex-slave educate his own heart, he tried to convey to his listeners the importance of their hearts as well. He taught that Philosophy was not merely a subject to be talked about, but was indeed a way of life. Epictetus' teaching heavily influenced the Roman Emperor Marcus Aurelius as he waged war with various nation-states throughout Southern Asia and Europe. Marcus Aurelius' military campaigns were largely responsible for the emergence of Europe as a continental world power until North America took over this role in the 19th century.

Although Alexander's worldwide conquests ended, Epictetus' teachings are still with us today and are used by many to build personal, organizational and national character. Just look at some of his well-known quotes:

- No man is free who is not master of himself
- Be careful to leave your sons well instructed rather than rich, for the hopes of the instructed are better than the wealth of the ignorant.
- It is impossible to begin to learn that which one thinks one already knows.
- It is the nature of the wise to resist pleasures, but the foolish to be a slave to them.

Although the life circumstances or life atmosphere for Alexander and Epictetus were polar opposites, they both came to be genuinely learned men. They were not of the learned gentry because they completed high school or college. They were learned men because they actively took their educations. These men changed and continue to change the world. Having a college degree may get someone a 9 to 5 accounting job, but taking a genuine education gives even the commonest of people the ability to enlarge their influence and change the world.

A Vision of a Better Life

Some may argue that Alexander the Great and Epictetus are ancient historical figures whose life details cannot be reliably known. Therefore any conclusions about the effect of education on their lives borders on conjecture. This argument is a reasonable one. So, to give a real-life, compelling example of how the taking of an education transcends a person's life atmosphere, consider Andrea McMiller's story, told in her own words.

As a child, I always envisioned a better life. My life's atmosphere was not a positive one. I was raised in the small town of Crawford, Alabama until I was four. I do not know how many people were living in Crawford when I was born, but in 2007, the population was only 3,200. When I lived there, the little town was nestled deep in the woods and had only one church and an old country store. The nearest hospital was in Tuskegee, over 30 miles away. Unfortunately, I was born into a family and social environment where education was not deemed important or even necessary. Although I was not a literal slave, I was fettered by poverty and caged in ignorance. My loving grandparents raised me and my two younger sisters. Although they did the best they could, my grandparents were not financially or socially equipped to raise young children. Both of them were physically ill, elderly and unable to work. Neither of them had ever learned to read or write. Of course, I do not begrudge them for this. Relatively high illiteracy rates have plagued Russell County, Alabama for quite some time now. My grandparents' only source of income was their monthly Social Security checks. There was never enough money to make ends meet.

I never knew my father and my mother was not consistently available for the greater part of my childhood. I grew up in relative social isolation. I do not remember thinking that my life was abnormal in any way. I did not realize how dreadfully poor I was or how devoid my life was of social stimulation, interacting only with my little sisters and my ailing grandparents. Then I started kindergarten. On my very first day of school, I saw the full extent of our poverty. The other children had decent clothes while mine were tattered and worn. The majority of the other kids had attended pre-K or were home schooled by their parents. They knew so much more than me. I distinctly remember feeling embarrassed. I was five years old and all I knew were my numbers, and those only to ten. I did not know the alphabet. I did not even understand the concept of school.

I was not only behind academically; I was behind socially as well. I was shy and awkward and stuck out like a sore thumb. I was ridiculed something awful. The other students called me dumb and stupid. After realizing how far behind I was, the teacher herself, Mrs. Black, called me dumb and stupid as well. Mrs. Black was my worst nightmare. Not many adults can recall details of their kindergarten year; but I do. I absolutely hated school. I spent the first half of my kindergarten year in mind-numbing terror. Fortunately, halfway into the school year Mrs. Black had become less malignant and I had grown accustomed to my environment. By the time I started the first grade, I knew that I wasn't stupid like Mrs. Black said I was. Yes, I was still awkward and shy but I clearly had a knack for learning. I think I enjoyed learning because it seemed fun to me. All the way to 6th grade, I excelled academically and remember being called one of the top students in my class.

Despite my being a top student, I was still teased for various reasons, sometimes for being too poor and other times for being too shy. The more I was teased the more I wanted to find a place to run and hide. I found none. But I did find solace and refuge in my studies. Because I did not have any friends to hang out with or to do my homework with, my study routine involved completing worksheets and vocabulary words at home in my room. I desperately longed for someone to help me with my homework or to just pat me on the back and say "good job, Andrea." But my home life just wasn't like that. To this day, I do not know why I started practicing my vocabulary and spelling words while standing in front of the mirror. But for whatever reason, I did and I liked doing it. Over the years, I have reflected on why I could have started this practice. The only thing that I have come up with is that by pretending to be the teacher, I somehow elevated myself above the cruel, ridicule of my classmates. After all, teachers were never ridiculed. The more I reviewed my homework in the mirror, the better I understood it. There were very few exams that I did not ace. Because I genuinely understood the material, I continued to excel academically.

Unfortunately, book sense did not translate into useful life experience. Because of my age-related social ignorance and lack of a family support, unimaginable things happened to me. At age 12, I was raped by a 22-year-old man and became pregnant. Now, if this violent crime had happened to a 12 year old girl in a more traditional family, the rapist would have been prosecuted and imprisoned. The rape victim would have been given familial, religious, psychological support to help cope with the psychological damage of the crime. Unfortunately, I did not come from a traditional family. The rapist was not jailed. I was not given familial, religious, social or any other support. Instead, my own mother forced me to marry and to live with the rapist as his child-bride. No, this is not a misprint and you are not in the Twilight Zone. You read correctly. At age 12, I was raped by a stranger, became pregnant as a result of the rape and was forced by my own mother to live with my rapist as his 12 year old wife. Apparently, my mother was more concerned with me not embarrassing the family by being an unwed, pregnant pre-teen.

This tragedy happened in the United States of America, not in some third world country with no rule of law. Of course, the rapist continued to abuse me as I was quite available to him. At least twice he beat me with his fists. Thank God, that this unimaginable, nightmarish torture that my mother called a marriage was short-lived. No force on earth could transform a child rapist into a husband, or a victimized child into an adoring wife. A couple of months after I gave birth to my son, the rapist finally left. Do not try to wrap your mind around this unbelievable situation. I have tried to make sense out of it for decades and still cannot. So, there I was, my childhood, gone; my situation, destitute. Being a pregnant 12-year-old in junior high school brought on even more ridicule and mockery than I had previously been subjected to. I retreated deeper into my school work. I continued pretending to be the teacher by teaching my homework lessons in the mirror.

Even with a fully gravid abdomen, I continued to go to school. As a matter of fact, I was sitting in class on the Friday before Christmas break in 1986 when my contractions kicked in. I had never felt such horrible pain in all my 12 short years of life. As each painful wave gripped my body, I braced myself the best way I could and tolerated the pain. My contractions continued for about a week, but were irregular. Then they became more regular and painful as I approached my 41st week of pregnancy. I remember someone telling me that water was supposed to gush out of me; but water never gushed out --- only blood. I told my mother and she took me to the hospital. For two days I labored in mind-numbing pain. I remember feeling embarrassed by the nurses and doctors' reactions when they learned that I was only 12. I was not given an epidural or any other pain medication. I was too young to know that I could have simply demanded pain medication. But how many 12 year olds would know to assert themselves in such a manner? Precious few, that's how many. On Thursday January 2, 1987 at about 1:14 PM, I had my son.

After giving birth, I was more determined than ever to overcome the negative aspects of my circumstances. Two weeks after giving birth, I was back in school ready to learn. Each day after school I would rock my son in one arm while I did my homework in the other. I still taught my homework in the mirror and quickly caught up in all my classes. Though I had always been an honor roll student, that semester I made straight A's. The next two years were difficult for me and my son. My financially-strapped grandparents had to provide food, diapers and clothing for my son. They simply did not have the financial means do so. So, at age 15 I lied about my age in order to get a job. But even as teen mom and child laborer, I still had a voracious appetite to learn. Because my grades remained stellar throughout high school, I was able to join several honor societies and other academic achievement clubs. I graduated from high school with honors, ranking in the top 10% of my class. I received an academic scholarship to the local community college. Yes, it was difficult balancing school, work and a toddler. Each time I got knocked down, I stood back up. I went on to Columbus State University in Columbus, GA and graduated with a B.A. in Criminal Justice. I still had a thirst for learning and earned my Master's Degree in Public Administration. So, despite my negative life atmosphere; I persevered and took my education.

Ordinary vs. Extraordinary

Notice the pattern in the lives of Alexander the Great, Epictetus and Andrea McMiller? I am not being gratuitous by placing McMiller in the company of Alexander the Great and Epictetus. All three lives were extraordinary in their own way. Alexander was tutored by the famous Aristotle and subsequently conquered the known world. Epictetus was born into slavery, had his leg broken to break his will to learn. But the slave freed himself from slavery and became a world renowned philosopher. McMiller was raped at age 12 and was forced to live with her rapist as his 12-year old bride, gave birth at 13 but then graduated from high school with honors, earned an academic scholarship, a Bachelors and Master's degree. All three lives were and are extraordinary. Despite a person's life atmosphere and circumstance, nearly anyone who lives into adulthood has the choice to be an ordinary or an extraordinary individual. One does not have to be in an extra-ordinary educational system in order to take an extra-ordinary education.

Yes. I am referring to the U.S. educational system here. At present, there is nothing extra-ordinary about it. I have gone through it. I see children and teenagers in it right now. Our school system has evolved not to impart a world-class education, but to merely acclimatize children to popular culture, giving them a place to go for five (or four) days a week for 12 years. If our school system was genuinely concerned with imparting a world-class education, our society would cherish teachers much like King Philip II cherished Aristotle. Teachers would be paid six figures instead of the paltry salaries that they make now. Furloughing teachers would be considered a near criminal act. Qualifications for remaining a teacher would be stringent and inextricably tied to student performance. Teachers and principals who allow students to cheat would promptly go to jail. Our curricula would be purpose-driven instead of political correctness-driven. Teachers and school boards would understand the uselessness of teaching students to simply pass tests. The singular objective of our schools would be to teach students how to become lifetime learners.

American schools are not currently poised to give our children world-class educations. Just look at our student's daily or quarterly routines. Students are collected in classrooms and presented with an assortment of facts to remember for regurgitation on multiple-choice exams a few weeks later. After eight to ten years of repeating this pattern, high schools issue 75% of their students a decorative diploma and proclaim them "high-school educated." The other 25% drop out and go on to eke out poverty-stricken lives. Many of the 75% who graduate go on to some form of post-secondary education institution, be it technical school, junior college or a traditional 4-year university. University students typically squander their freshman years partying or otherwise enjoying the new freedoms that come with being an independent adult. By their sophomore and junior years they have started thinking seriously about their post-college careers and commit themselves to regular study. But the only way they know how to study is by doing the same thing they did in high school, re-read lecture notes, skim the textbook and highlight the important stuff. By the time they are college seniors, they have managed to get their grade point average to some respectable number. They graduate and enter the work force in a field that may have very little to do with their college degrees.

So, what percentage of American adults are we talking about here? What percentage of American actually has college degrees? We have already seen where the US lags behind other developed countries in high school academic achievement. When we compare the education attainment of international adults between age 25 and 64, as of 2009, fifty four percent of Russians have associate's degrees or higher. Canada is in second place with 48.3 % (Lee, 2010). United States trails at 34.9% (U.S. Census Bureau, 2009). But this was not always the case. In the 1980's the United States led the world in percent of the population with college degrees. But in 2010, the US ranks 12th among 36 developed nations. Although 12th of 36 is not a dismal ranking, it is certainly not characteristic of the United States.

But there is a deeper issue here. What does it matter that one nation has a higher or lower percentage of its citizens with college degrees? What does it really mean to have a college degree anyway? Remember when we were being hypothetical and compared contemporary top-performing American high school students to the teenaged Alexander the Great? I questioned our brightest student's ability to intelligently discuss current political events, discuss the events in the US from 1861-1865 or to identify China on an unlabeled map. The question now is, have these high school students developed a broader fund of knowledge about their own country and world geography after completing four years of college?

Recall that life atmosphere is determined by the complex interaction of a person's birth era, race, gender, family structure, socio-economic class and culture. Some people's life atmosphere facilitates their taking an education while other people's life atmosphere hinders the process. In a May 15, 2011 CNN documentary on education in America called "Don't Fail Me," host Soledad O'Brien reported disheartening facts. She reported that American high school students currently rank 17th of 34 in science and 24th of 34 in math, compared to other countries. The documentary compared the high school curricula of American students to high school curricula in other countries. In other countries, students do not have the choice to opt out of higher math and science. But in the US, students can choose to avoid higher math and science courses. And a significant proportion of them do just that.

Japanese high school students out-rank American students in both math and science. The life atmospheres of typical Japanese students are fundamentally different from those of American students. For Japanese students, cognitive engagement in math and science is extremely important to them. Their family life and parental expectations dictate highly structured, disciplined study habits at home. The unlimited watching of celebrity and reality TV shows and hanging out at the mall is the exception rather than the rule. For American students, the opposite is true. Our students have a great deal of unstructured time. Our students seem to be obsessed with and emulate physically attractive, but dim-witted celebrities and reality TV personalities. As sad as these facts may seem, what's even sadder is that they are indeed facts.

Unfortunately, some of our national politicians choose not to deal in facts. Instead they prefer to bask in blind American exceptionalism, believing that the US is more advanced in every aspect than every other nation on earth. They do not like to hear about our country's shortcomings. The ultra-conservative, Newt Gingrich is one such politician with this national perception illness. He loves to tickle the ears of friendly audiences by coaxing them to believe that America is exceptional in all that we do. Mr. Gingrich and like-minded politicians cause deep damage to our country by robbing us of the sense of urgency required to re-establish our intellectual leadership in the world. Independently researched facts seem to be unimportant to Gingrich-type politicians. While our educational system may have been exceptional a few decades ago, it is certainly not exceptional now. Which fact-based premises support my conclusion?

Premise 1: Since the beginning of the 21st century, American high school students rank progressively lower than other developed countries in math, science, reading and problem solving. In 2003, our 15 year olds ranked 24th of 38 in math, 19th of 38 in science, 12th of 38 in reading and 26th of 38 in problem solving (NCES , 2005). A repeat country comparison survey was done three years later, this time 57 countries were compared. In 2006, our 15 year olds ranked 29th of 57 in science and 35th of 57 in math. (Organization for Economic Co-operation & Development OCED).

Premise 2: In almost all U.S. high schools, many middle schools and some elementary schools Asian and well-to-do white students dominate (are tracked into or strive to get into) the higher math and science classes (Hochschild, 2003). However, there is "a pervasive and ever-growing student achievement gap with minority and poor students clustered in the lower tiers while white and Asian students occupy the higher tiers" (Montgomery County Education Forum MCEF, 2002). Table 1 is a summary of outcome measures as evidence of the academic achievement gap among Asian, white, black and Latino students in the Montgomery County Public Schools. This data is representative of achievement gap trends throughout the United States.

Table 1
Tracking the Achievement Gap in Montgomery, Alabama Schools

Indicator	Asian	White	Black	Latino	Gap
Ave. SAT score	1131	1149	922	973	193
Participation in Honors & AP (%)	69.2	64.6	30.3	30.9	36
Participation in Pre-Algebra (%)	53.3	45.0	14.4	12.7	36
Completed Algebra by 9th Grade (%)	86.4	85.5	48.6	44.3	40
Participates in PSATs (%)	73	73	40	29	39
Over-Representation in Special Education	0.85	4.33	5.80	4.83	2.7
Suspension Rate	2.7	4.1	11.7	7.1	6

Premise 3: The racial demographic of the US is rapidly changing. Shortly after 2020, and for the first time in US history, minority

students will out-number white students on college campuses (Chronicle Research Services, 2010). These are the same minority students who have historically occupied the bottom tiers of academia in our public schools.

There is absolutely nothing exceptional about our current education system. We can choose to become emotionally upset and hence, distracted by the racial disparities in student performance. We can also be like the Gingrich-type politicians and maintain that our educational system is still exceptional despite clear evidence that it is not. But becoming upset or burying our heads in the sand contributes to the political inertia that prevents us from overhauling our education system at national, state and local levels. But all is not lost. We can once again condition young American minds to become analytical, investigative and creators of multi-dimensional solutions for our multi-dimensional problems. The first step to re-vitalizing our country's intellectualism is to stop becoming so defensive whenever we are presented facts. The United States is an exceptional country, not because we merely think so, but because of our history of self-sacrifice and dogged determination in the face of staggering odds. More than any other nation on earth, the United States, with all of its struggles, gifts and triumphs is an extraordinary nation.

In 1963, Martin Luther King Jr. said that he dreamed that "one day this nation will rise up and live out the true meaning of its creed." What creed? The American creed is not merely a colloquialism that sounds good in a speech. It is actually a formal document adopted by the US House of Representatives on April 3, 1918. This is the American Creed:

> I believe in the United States of America, as a government of the people, by the people, for the people; whose just powers are derived from the consent of the governed; a democracy in a republic; a sovereign Nation of many sovereign States; a perfect union, one and inseparable; established upon those principles of freedom, equality, justice, and humanity for which American patriots sacrificed their lives and fortunes. I therefore believe it is my duty to my country to love it, to support its Constitution, to obey its laws, to respect its flag, and to defend it against all enemies (Page, 1918).

Notice the clause "a democracy in a republic." Living out the true meaning of our country's creed means that we must remain a democratic republic, basically a representative government where the majority rules. The only way to live out this clause is by investing heavily in education. President Thomas Jefferson wrote that "if a nation expects to be ignorant and free, it expects what never was and never will be." Never in human history has a nation of poorly educated citizens remained a free people. Even now, in the US, we have tended away from genuine democracy with a constitutionally protected system of checks and balances toward an oligarchy, which is a government run by a few wealthy individuals (or corporations). So while we ordinary Americans let our iPads and smart phones think for us, we lose more and more of our country's governing power to fewer and fewer wealthy individuals or corporations. As long as we rest on our laurels and get angry when we are told that our nation is not exceptional, we contribute to our transformation from a democratic republic to some lesser form of government.

Americans must start being extraordinary again. And to be extraordinary, we must stop doing ordinary things. Perhaps the most important time in our lives to be extraordinary is when we are still in *student status*. You do not have to be enrolled in an academic institution to be in student status. By *student status*, I mean keeping your mind open and receptive of new ideas and uncharted possibilities. The best Kung Fu masters remain students of the art indefinitely. The best college professors remain able to glean new perspectives from the greenest of freshmen. It is only when we think we have universal answers that we become rigid and intolerant of other people and other people's ideas. The iTeachMe method can help ordinary students become extraordinary ones. Extraordinary does not mean complicated. Actually, extraordinary people have a knack for making the complicated seem simple to others. iTeachMe is a simple study method. The most efficient way to retain new concepts is to teach them to someone else. But, you cannot teach what you do not understand. The iTeachMe study method allows students to continually assess their understanding of newly integrated concepts by requiring students to teach these concepts on a regular basis.

The iTeachMe method is not new; variations of the method can be seen throughout history and in many civilizations. Goal-directed interrogation, also known as the Socratic Method is a form of iTeachMe. Earlier, we learned how Germany re-discovered the ancient Socratic Method and re-packaged it as their *Lernen durch Lehren* or "learn by teach" method. Throughout the first five books of the Old Testament, the Israelites were commanded to teach various community and religious laws to their young children throughout the course of each day. Of course, young children could not understand complicated social and religious laws. But what better way to instill the Law into the parent's long-term memory than by requiring them to teach it often? The Israelites were not given a list of life circumstances for with they could skip their teaching responsibility. The parents' individual life atmospheres were generally irrelevant. They were commanded to teach their youngsters daily and they did just that.

So, we see that the student may not be the primary beneficiary of teaching. The teacher benefits as well. Now imagine removing the student all together. The teacher still benefits from teaching. Why is a student audience necessary? It was not necessary for me when I taught Physiology to my pillow or when Andrea McMiller taught her homework in the mirror. This is the reason that the iTeachMe method is so named and the reason why iTeachMe is an improvement over Germany's *Lernen durch Lehren* Method. The iTeachMe method does not require an audience and lends itself particularly well to portability. iTeachMe students can teach themselves in the privacy of their own homes or wherever else they choose to establish their personal teaching environment.

Chapter 2
How We Learn

It is no secret; people learn in different ways. Everyone has a learning style. By "learning style," I specifically mean a unique set of preferences for gathering and processing new information. A person's learning style may be associated with his or her intelligence level. People who can quickly integrate new information into their existing knowledge base are usually considered "intelligent" by others. The same goes for individuals who can easily integrate new skills to their existing skill set; they are said to have a "natural talent" in that activity. Education researchers have long been interested in figuring out the many ways that people learn. This type of research has given rise to various types of learning theories. Perhaps the most well-known learning theory researcher is Dr. Neil D. Fleming. After decades of teaching and observing students in the classroom, Dr. Fleming defined four learning styles, Visual, Auditory, Reading (and Writing) and Kinesthetic. He coined the acronym, VARK and in 1987 developed a questionnaire designed to classify individuals into one or more VARK categories. (Fleming, 1992)

The VARK model is one of the most commonly cited models in education research. Fleming holds that visual learners learn best by looking at diagrams, pictures, charts or films. These learners also tend to:

- take detailed notes
- sit in the front of the class to better see the board
- be neat and tidy
- close their eyes to visualize or remember something
- find something to watch if they are bored
- need to see what they are learning

Auditory learners learn best by hearing. They benefit from traditional teaching methods such as lectures and presentations. These learners readily grasp instruction when they are read aloud. Other attributes of auditory learners include:

- a tendency to sit where they can hear but not having a need to pay attention to what is happening in front
- decreased ability to coordinate colors or clothing, but can explain why they choose the colors or clothing that they did
- humming or talking to themselves or others when bored

Students who learn best by reading and writing have an overwhelming need to see or produce written words. People who prefer this learning modality are often addicted to PowerPoint, make lots of lists, and frequently consult dictionaries, thesauri and quotation books. Finally, kinesthetic or tactile learners learn by doing things. Fleming's research showed that kindergarten children tended to learn best by kinesthetic means, like feeling, touching and physically experiencing the subject matter. He observed that as kindergartners entered the second and third grades, many became visual learners. Later, in the fifth and sixth grades, female students tended to morph into auditory learners while male students maintained kinesthetic proclivities throughout their lives.

Although Fleming's VARK model is widely accepted, it grossly underestimates a person's ability to learn. The human brain or mind operates on multiple levels and in different dimensions all at the same time. It is not limited to processing information within strict VARK categories. Fleming suggests that the brain is thus limited. He even offers for sale an online VARK questionnaire for people to purchase if they want to find out which type of VARK learner they are. This model conveys the idea of exclusivity, as if a learning style is some innate trait, like eye color or height. But isn't it possible for, say a kinesthetic learner to naturally shift into visual, reading or auditory modes as necessary? I say, absolutely! Just like it is possible for people who prefer eating with chopsticks to also eat with a spoon, kinesthetic learners can also learn via other modalities too.

We do not learn just by hearing, seeing, writing or doing. Our brain processes information by doing all of the above at the same time. Whatever method or combination of methods the brain uses to learn, one thing is for sure, the brain always tries to attach meaning to any knowledge that will be stored long term. This is why the rote memorization of unrelated facts almost never stays in our long-term memory. We dump meaningless or confusing information because our minds have a need to arrange our experiences in simple, logical patterns. This experience-organizing tendency is the very definition of the word "sanity." One sure way to organize conceptual data into coherent constructs is to simply teach it. In order to do this, the teacher's brain must combine several of Fleming's VARK learning styles together and operate within them simultaneously. Not only do teachers need to use their visual, auditory, verbal and kinesthetic abilities to explain concepts logically, but they also have to manage their own psychological responses to the students during the process.

During the teaching process, the brain pulls from its visual, auditory and written language centers to build a coherent picture of a concept in someone else's mind. The structure of the brain and its tendency to process information in broad or holistic terms makes it an excellent "teaching machine." This is why the act of teaching is the best method for learning. The ancient philosophers knew this. There is plenty of psychological research that demonstrate the brain's natural tendency to process information holistically, instead of through separate visual, auditory, language or kinesthetic channels. In German psychology, Gestaltism is the theory that the human mind-brain is a holistic entity with self-organizing tendencies. The word "Gestalt" actually means "the essence or shape of an entity's complete form" (Hothersall, 2004). The word was first introduced by the German psychologist, Christian von Ehrenfels. In plain terms, the "Gestalt effect" is the ability of our brain to use all of its spatial-visual, reasoning, auditory and emotional abilities to paint a coherent picture.

The phrase "The whole is greater than the sum of its parts" is often used when explaining Gestalt theory. The iTeachMe study method is built on Gestalt theory. There are several tenants or principles of Gestaltism, including the principles of Totality, Rectification and Multi-stability. We will consider each of these principles individually to see how they manifest themselves in the iTeachMe method. Do not worry that you do not know how to do the iTeachMe method yet. You will learn that in Chapter 5.

Figure 2.1
Gestalt Principle of Totality

Look at this picture. What do you see? Many people will not immediately recognize the Dalmatian dog, sniffing the leaves next to a shade tree. But once they do recognize the dog, they do not perceive the dog in separate parts. In other words the mind does not build the image of the dog by first perceiving the dog's leg, head or tail, then inferring from these parts the whole image of the dog. Instantly, at the moment of perception, the dog comes into the mind's eye. Your mind has a need to make sense out of confusion. Your mind does not do this only when looking at pictures. Your mind tries to do this every moment of every day. When you learn new concepts, you are learning isolated information. While you may initially understand the details of the concept being taught, you will likely forget this new information unless you insert the information into a broader framework of existing knowledge. When you learn the individual iTeachMe steps in chapter five, you will learn that each teaching hour begins with the student writing their outline on the lecture chart prior to teaching. By teaching to an outline, the student conditions their mind to accept and store new concepts in a logical manner.

Figure 2.2
Gestalt Principle of Rectification

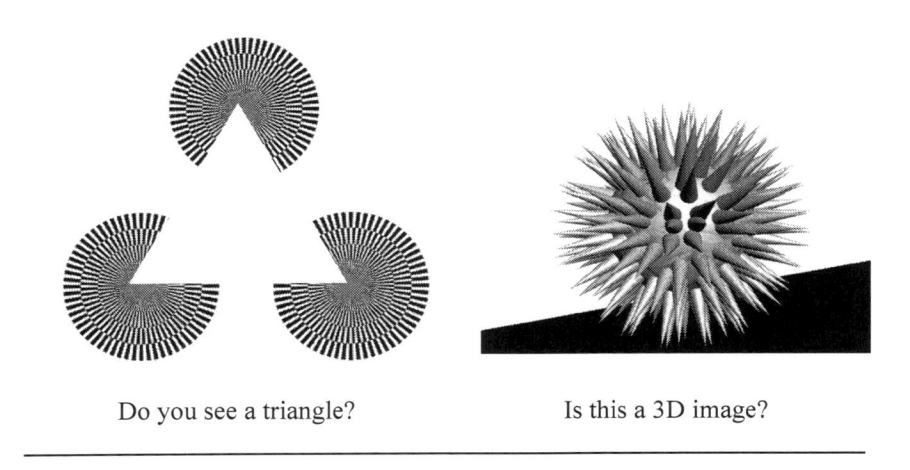

Do you see a triangle?   Is this a 3D image?

The word *rectification* literally means "to put right" or "to make correct." Of course, the terms "right" and "correct" may mean different things to different people. But there are many situations in life where the notion of "correctness" is shared by nearly everyone. This is the only reason that magic tricks work. Nearly everyone knows that it is incorrect or impossible to pull a living rabbit out of a hat that the magician was just wearing. So, when the magician pulls the rabbit out, he violates the audience's notion of "correctness" or their beliefs about what makes sense in the world. Magicians actually depend on their audiences to make logical connections or assumptions. Otherwise, no one would be surprised when the magician performs tricks that violate the laws of nature. Magicians living in Alice's Wonderland would never find work. In Wonderland, everything is fantasy; nothing is supposed to make sense.

The mind makes connections that are not actually there. Look at the three Pac man figure in the "Rectification" box above. Although no triangle is drawn, your mind infers one. Look at the image to the right of the Pac man configuration. It appears that the sphere has sharp spikes coming out of the page. The image appears to be a 3-dimensional image. But isn't the term 3-dimensional image an oxymoron? All images must be drawn on a 2-dimensional page. How can any image drawn in two dimensions appear 3-dimensional? You can see a triangle and a 3-dimensional image in Figure 2.2 because your mind cannot help but to form logical connections in its never-ending quest to organize information in a logical manner.

Our brains are truly remarkable. Some psychology researchers often use the term mind-brain to acknowledge the mystery of how the mind and the brain are actually connected. No one knows how the brain gives rise to the mind. Of course, we know that one cannot have a mind without a brain, but plenty of people can have a brain without evidence of having a working mind. Coma victims on life support may be a good example. We also know that there is a direct correlation between the degree of neuronal connections within the brain and the sophistication of the mind. This is why a 5 year old child cannot interpret the old saying, "people who live in glass houses shouldn't throw stones." The 5 year olds' neuronal connections or higher reasoning abilities are quite limited compared to a 28 year old's. A child cannot think in abstract terms like the adult can. The child would try to interpret the above proverb in concrete terms by saying that the walls of the glass house would break if the occupant threw a stone. A psychologically normal adult would immediately recognize the figurativeness of this proverb and give the correct moral interpretation of "don't be a hypocrite."

Why can adults think in the abstract, while children cannot? What is the difference between the adult and the child's brain? An adult's brain is larger than a child's. By larger, I mean has more volume. The adult's brain has more neural connections or synapses than the child's. It seems that the more neural connections the brain makes, the more abstract cognitive ability it has. No one can argue that the mind is greater than the collection of the 100 billion neurons that make up the brain. Traditional neuroscience holds that we humans are born with all 100 billion neurons (individual nerve cells) that we will ever have. Yes, throughout childhood our neurons reproduce themselves, grow longer tails and develop a fatty sheath along their tails to optimize signal transmission. It has been long held by the scientific community that after childhood neurons stop reproducing themselves. However, current research has found that neurons in the hippocampi of primates actually do reproduce themselves far beyond childhood (Gross, 2000).

But is there a direct correlation between cognitive ability and hippocampal volume? Maybe there is. But let's not just focus on the hippocampus. After all, the hippocampus is just a part of a larger brain system called the limbic system. Other well-known components of the limbic system include the amygdala and the nucleus accumbens (the pleasure center). There are still other components of the limbic system, but discussing them here would be beyond the scope of this book. For purposes of our discussion, it is sufficient for you to know that the limbic system is the deep core part of the brain where our emotional responses and memories of sensory stimulation interface. "Our limbic system is what gets duped when people get addicted to hard drugs" (Anissimov, 2011). I know--- all of this neuroscience talk can get too technical. So, let me put the limbic system's role in learning into practical perspective here. The limbic system, not only stores our long-term memories, but also connects these memories to specific emotions.

This system is the reason why we have pleasure and fear, likes, dislikes, favorites and worsts.

To see the limbic system at work, take a look at the image in the box below. What do you see? Let me remind you that the Gestalt theory of rectification holds that your mind has a strong need to make logical sense out of fragmented information to form a holistic picture. In the box below, there is no water drawn, not even a shimmer of a wave. But your mind puts water there. Also, your mind instantly concluded that there is only one sea creature when there could easily be two or three. The first creature could be showing its head and neck, while the second and third creatures could be showing the middle body loop and the tail respectively. Only now do you acknowledge the possibility of several creatures being present, but your mind did not first assume this.

Figure 2.3
Simultaneous Cognitive Operations

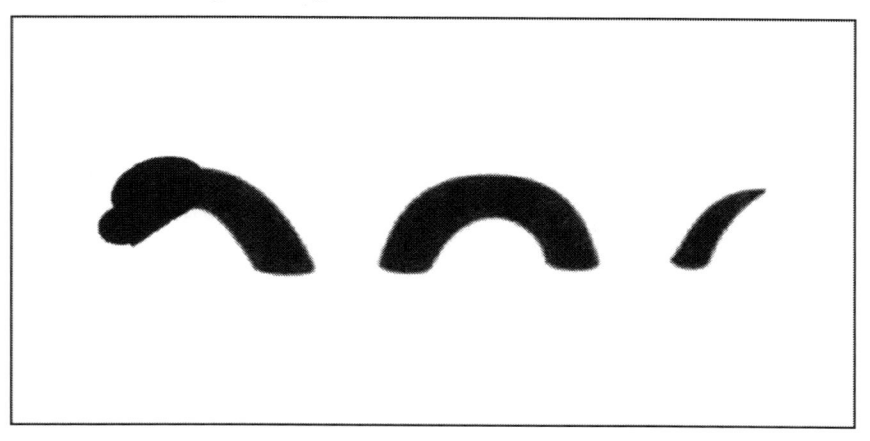

This is another example of plain old Gestalt rectification, where your mind makes logical connections that are not actually there. But your mind does more than just make connections by inserting water or connecting a disjointed body. Your limbic system is at work here too. It stirred up some long-term memories which are also glued to a specific emotional response. The drawing above probably conjures up memories of the Loch Ness monster, especially if you are from Scotland or the United Kingdom. But even if you are not from the UK and have never heard of the Loch Ness monster, you are still likely to have some type of memory-emotion response to this creature. Still not convinced? Then just answer these questions truthfully. If this sea creature was real, would you get into the water and take a skinny dip alongside it? Would you prod and poke it with your finger? Of course not! But why wouldn't you? There is a very specific reason why you would not --- fear.

Do you see what your limbic system has done here? It has informed your higher brain, your frontal cortex, that this monster is probably much bigger than a tadpole and probably much bigger than you. You have had a lifetime of experiences (memories) of potentially dangerous situations that you now know to avoid. You would not knowingly put yourself into a dangerous situation. A newborn baby would swim next to this Loch Ness monster with absolutely no fear. The newborn's limbic system has not had the time to associate past memories with noxious stimuli like the pain of being bitten, stung or viciously attacked by a ferocious leviathan.

I think it is pretty clear now that the limbic system is the deep, core part of the brain that attaches our experiences (memories) to specific emotions. When our emotions run high, our long-term memory becomes near photographic, like a genius. This is why many people can recall precise details of what they were doing when some emotionally-charged event happens. What were you doing at 8:45 AM September 11, 2001 or at 12:30 PM November 22, 1963? The same reason that your memory seems clear on the morning of 9-11 or on the afternoon when President John F. Kennedy got shot is the same reason that students can remember math problems that they had to explain while standing in front of the class. Increased emotional tone improves the long-term memory. For most people, speaking in front of a group or teaching a concept to someone else increases their emotional tone, i.e. causes apprehension. When a student is asked to stand up in front of the class and explain a concept, that student is likely to have a heightened emotional response. That student may feel some angst or nervousness about making incorrect statements. The heart rate increases and the throat narrows. That student will either display more caution in explaining the concept or find some way to get off the hot seat, perhaps with a joke. Whatever the outcome, this student will remember many details about this brief moment on the hot seat. But see, this is where the secret of intellectual prowess lies --- on the hot seat. Students can take the "hot seat" experience home to their living rooms or bedrooms. They can take advantage of their limbic system's ability to store new concepts directly into their long-term memories by using the iTeachMe method to teach their homework lessons to others or to themselves.

We started this chapter by discussing Dr. Fleming's VARK learning styles. We ended by explaining how the mind-brain is extremely dynamic and capable of learning on many levels and in different dimensions all at the same time. The least that you should remember in this chapter is that any learning theory worth its salt simply must take the limbic system into account. This is why teaching a subject to other people is the most efficient way to transfer information from the short-term to the long-term memory.

Chapter 3
...and the Band Played On

Shortly after midnight, as Titanic's lifeboats had begun to be loaded, Wallace Hartley assembled his band in the First Class Lounge, where many of the First Class passengers were now assembling, and began to play. Many people later commented on how strange it seemed to be wearing a life jacket, awaiting orders to get into the lifeboats, whilst the band continued to play away as though nothing had happened. Later, as more and more people began to realize the seriousness of the situation, and began to file onto the Boat Deck, so too did Hartley, reassembling his men on the Boat Deck close to the entrance of the Grand Staircase.

Many people are of the opinion that the actions of Wallace Hartley and the other members of Titanic's band in the time between the collision and the final foundering kept passengers calm, and enabled the lifeboats to be loaded in an orderly fashion, which may be correct. There is of course another school of thought; that people on board the doomed liner didn't realize the seriousness of the situation soon enough because of the music the band played (Carroll, 2002).

Vaunted by the White Star Line, an English shipping company, as the grandest of all luxury liners, an utterly unsinkable ship, the Titanic hit an iceberg late night April 14, 1912 and sank in the freezing Atlantic Ocean within three hours. Of the 2,228 people aboard, there were only enough lifeboats aboard to hold one-half of the passengers. Before the Titanic left England, the crew found it unnecessary to bring the full complement of lifeboats aboard. After all, the luxury liner was unsinkable. The above excerpt is a re-telling of the last few hours of the band leader, Wallace Hartley's life while aboard the doomed ocean liner. While we cannot know exactly what was going through Hartley's mind or if he even knew that he and his band were doomed, it is a commonly-held belief that he was indeed well aware of his plight. Hartley's knowledge of his impending doom and his subsequent decision to keep the band playing is actually the reason why he is celebrated. This is where the phrase --- *and the band played on* comes from. What is astonishing about the band playing on is that with no hope of survival, Hartley and the band members resolved within their hearts not spend their last hour in a frenzied panic but to sink to their freezing, watery grave gracefully. That is why the band played on.

Allow me to compare the U.S. education system to the unsinkable Titanic. A few loose analogies can certainly be made. Remember our discussion about blind American exceptionalism? People who suffer from blind exceptionalism usually reject any form of evidence that paints the US in a less than exceptional light. Of course, we should all have a healthy sense of national pride. However, we must not delude ourselves. In the areas where we are verifiably exceptional, we should proclaim it on every rooftop. But in the areas where we are slipping or are not exceptional, we must examine ourselves and improve. At his trial for heresy, Socrates said that the unexamined life is not worth living. Indeed, the unexamined country is not worth living in. Having a sense of blind exceptionalism is damaging to our posterity. Believe it or not, there are actually some Americans who still think that our education system is the best in the world. These people are like the English shipping company, White Star Line, who vaunted the Titanic as an unsinkable ship.

Our education system is our Titanic; and our Titanic is sinking. But unlike the situation on the real Titanic, our plight is not hopeless. We can save American education. We can get back to the top of international academic performance rankings. Despite all of the signs that our system is getting worse, we have not shown the willingness to save it. Like Hartley's band, we have seemingly resolved to continue business as usual, as if nothing catastrophic is happening. Throughout the country, our teachers teach the same old pre-fabricated curricula year after year. Teachers do not have time to actually teach to the student's understanding, so instead teach to the test, giving subtle hints about which material will appear on upcoming exams. Teachers teach to tests in order to avoid their own negative performance evaluations that usually follow their students' poor test performances. We double down on the same old failed education policies at the state and federal levels. We do these things all while our students sink lower and lower into an abyss of indifference, ignorance and intellectual mediocrity.

Why is it such a big deal that we sank from the upper ranks to the middle and lower ranks in science and math? It is a big deal because this academic decline mirrors an intellectual degradation that is rapidly spreading throughout the country. Ever wonder why the fictional characters Homer Simpson and Peter Griffin remain popular American icons? They are illustrated as the typical American dad, with big bellies and little intelligence. In 2006 French neurologists published a research study that showed a direct correlation between obesity and decreased cognitive function in healthy but sedentary adults (Cournot, 2006). Many in the scientific community promptly called this phenomenon the Homer Simpson effect. What is interesting is that in 2009 the U.S Postal Service celebrated Homer Simpson as an American icon and prominently displayed him with his oversized belly on a U.S.

stamp. Some may argue that Homer Simpson and Peter Griffin's popularity does not mean that our country celebrates idiocy. After all, they are just fictional, illustrated characters.

So, if our enduring fascination with dim witted cartoon characters is not a harbinger of doom for the country, then what about our fascination with real life people? What kind of people intrigue or mesmerize us? Who do we celebrate? The answer is easy---our celebrities. The very definition of the word *celebrity* is a person whose life we celebrate. And quite naturally, young people in our society, in any society, will emulate celebrated people. Now there is a difference between being a celebrity and being well-known or recognizable. Osama Bin Laden was quite recognizable, but he was not a celebrity. Nobody celebrated him, at least not here in the US. Yes, celebrities are well-known and recognizable, but they are also celebrated and emulated by others. Which well-known people do Americans celebrate and emulate? Just turn on your TV and flip through the channels. We celebrate the Lindsay Lohan, Paris Hilton, and the Kim Kardashian-type people. They captivate us, hold our attention, and are the subject of conversations throughout the country.

Why do we celebrate them? What positive thing do they contribute to our society that is not smoke and mirrors, court-ordered community service or reputation-repairing activities? They contribute nothing of genuine substance. They actually damage our society by promoting superficiality, pulling our adolescent girls away from genuine psycho-social development toward mindless materialism. Why do I assume that these *celebrities* are not psycho-socially developed? Well, psycho-socially developed women do not compete for media attention by repeatedly driving drunk, flashing bared vaginas or peddling their sex tapes like a commodity on the open market.

Not only are many American women consumed with celebrities, but many are also addicted to mindless reality shows. Their daily routines are generally devoid of intellectually stimulating activities. They rush home from work and stay glued to shows like Love and Hip Hop until they log onto Facebook to gossip about which girl is having sex with which rapper. Or they faithfully catch every episode of Bad Girls Club, anxious to see which girl can be the most outrageous, the most destructive, or have casual sex with the most guys. Our women are increasingly adopting the same empty materialistic values that Reality TV women portray. Trying to figure out solutions to actual problems in the world around them does not even register on their "things-I-like-to-do" meter. What does register is getting a Hermes Birkin or Gucci bag, buying red-bottom shoes; or watching the next episode of Housewives of [whatever city]. This is complete and utter madness. There is clearly a downhill progression here, away from intellectualism and toward mindlessness. Our country is sinking; a catastrophe is underway --- and the band plays on.

America's march toward intellectual lethargy is even worse for minorities, especially the black community. In nearly every urban center in the United States, little black boys are bombarded with images of flashy rappers with sagging pants, unlaced shoes and gold teeth. Black males of all ages only make up 6-7% of the U.S. population. It is difficult to find more than a handful of black teenagers in any location who have not adopted a rapper-like self-identity in their style of dress or manner of speech. The rapper or thug-identity does not promote academic excellence. Intellectuals are generally seen as nerds, geeks or otherwise un-cool. Those young black males who adopt rapper-like self-identities are less likely to grow up to become physicians, engineers or mathematicians. Historically, they do not end up as pillars of their families, leaving their women to raise children in fatherless homes. This socially destructive pattern has long been grappled with by many prominent black intellectuals, including Jawanza Kunjufu, who wrote that,

> Black males are caught in a self-perpetuating cycle of failure, in which the absence of stable, successful adult role models ensures that young blacks will do poorly in school, turn to street life, and father yet another generation of boys without adequate male role models. The net result is the prevention of black males from attaining positions of social and economic power (Kunjufu, 1982).

When black men are absent from the home, single black women have a greater responsibility to mitigate the negative effects of fatherlessness and the adoption of the thug identity. If the single black mother just so happen to be of the Gucci-bag chasing mentality, then her children will certainly observe this behavior and develop a similar set of values. Remember that as Americans, these children are still being influenced by ditsy celebrities and flashy rappers from whom they learn specific patterns of behaviors. It is these family/community challenges that contribute to our nation's intellectual decline.

But this decline is not a racial thing. It is a choice thing. How each of us chooses to live our lives determines America's collective consciousness or national character. Yes, each of us is free to whittle away our time watching reality TV or collecting more and more stuff. We do not think that our choices mean anything significant or say anything about our core selves. Of course, we do not take reality TV personalities seriously; at times, we just enjoy mindless entertainment like Jerry Springer or Bad Girls Club. They serve as a distraction from the seriousness of our daily lives. But this is the mistake. We can think that our everyday choices are a reflection of our personal preferences that stem from our individual freedoms. But, the choices we make are actually determined by powers far beyond our control. Brigid C. Harrison, a political science professor at Montclair State University wrote that,

> Ordinary men and women are driven by forces in society that they neither understand nor control. These forces are embodied in governmental authorities, economic organizations and markets, social value and ideologies, accepted ways of life, and learned patterns of behavior. However diverse the nature of these forces, they have in common the ability to modify the conduct of individuals, to control their behavior, and to shape their lives (Harrison, 2008)

So while we are free to watch what we want, dress like we want, buy what we want, our choices reflect our shared values as a nation. These shared values are given to us, modeled by the very people we choose to celebrate. The Titanic is sinking---and the band plays on. When a ship is lost at sea or is on the brink of disaster, the captain sends out an S.O.S or distress signal. S.O.S means *Save Our Ship* or *Save Our Souls*. For our purposes of our discussion, S.O.S means *Save Our Schools*. When a ship sends out an S.O.S call, they are asking for help. However, their asking for help does not decrease their responsibility to keep looking for ways to save themselves. The Titanic was doomed. The band's decision to play on was a resolution to die with dignity. Although our education system is sinking, it is by no means doomed. We have more than enough proverbial life boats to let down to save everyone onboard. We simply must put our instruments aside and get busy letting down life boats. We must change the basic structure of our education system. Who are the *we* that I'm referring to here? We are the federal and state government; we are the school boards and teachers; we are the parents; we are the students.

The Structure & Function of American Education

Since we are talking about saving our education system by changing its basic structure, we should first look at what this basic structure is. From kindergarten all the way up to graduate school, our classrooms have the same operational structure. Students assemble in large rooms to passively absorb bits of information put out by teachers. Yes, there are some environmental layout differences at the ends of the grade spectrum. Kindergarten classrooms are peppered with bright pictures that appeal to little inquisitive minds; university lecture halls are Spartan with symmetric rows of tiered seats and no pictures. But both classroom set ups place the teacher or professor prominently in the front, doling out information like an omniscient oracle of truth. Why do we arrange our classrooms / lecture halls like this? Did we spend decades doing research to find which type of set-up best facilitated learning? How do we even know that putting a teacher in the front to dole out information to relatively passive students is an effective way to pass on knowledge? The answers --- we don't. Our schools are set up like they are simply because this is the way we have always done things.

Much like Fleming's rigid VARK learning styles became a ubiquitous standard without much randomized controlled psychological research, teaching styles became widely disseminated without the benefit of long-term, verifiable research. Throughout the US, secondary and post-secondary educators strive to teach students using the authoritative model. But just look at where this teaching model came from. In the early 1960's, Dr.

Diana Baumrind, a clinical and developmental Psychologist conducted a few observational studies of how mothers interacted with their toddlers. She watched over 100 pre-school aged children interact with their mothers and from this, defined three parenting styles, authoritative, authoritarian, and permissive. These parenting styles were defined by the variable presence of two factors, parental demands on the child and parental responsiveness to the child's needs. Parents who demanded a lot from their children, like obedience, respect, and attention were said to have high *demandingness*. Parents who nurtured and were very attentive to their children were said to have high responsiveness. Varying combinations of high and low demands and responsiveness defined the three parenting styles. The three charts below summarize Dr. Baumrind's parenting styles.

Chart 3.1
Baumrind's Parenting Styles

Parental **Demands** placed on the child (obedience, respect, etc)

Parental **Responsiveness** to the child (feedback, praise, nurturing)

Authoritarian Parenting Style

- High parental demand
- Low parental responsiveness
- Rely on punishment
- Parent is dictator-like
- *Child is given Orders*

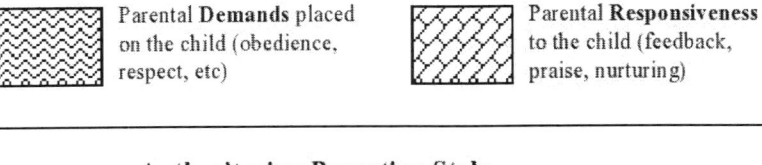

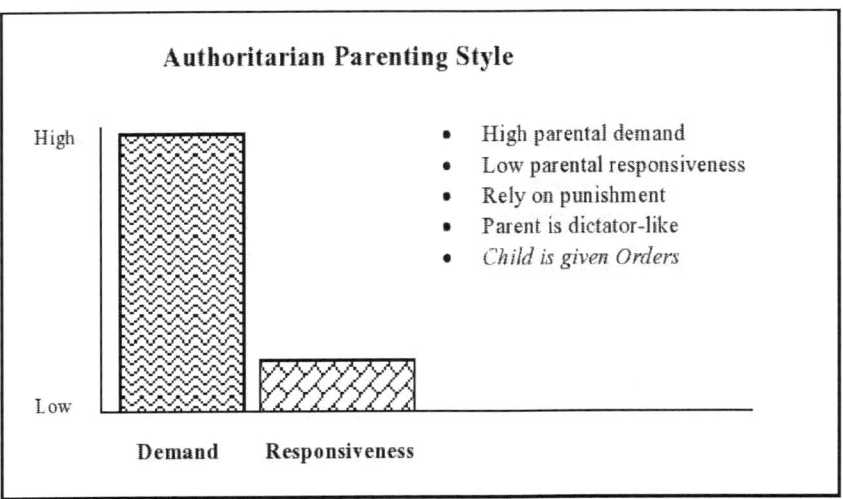

Authoritative Parenting Style

- High parental demand
- High parental responsiveness
- Supportive, warm environment
- Respect child's independence
- Explicit expectations given
- *Child is given choices*

Permissive Parenting Style

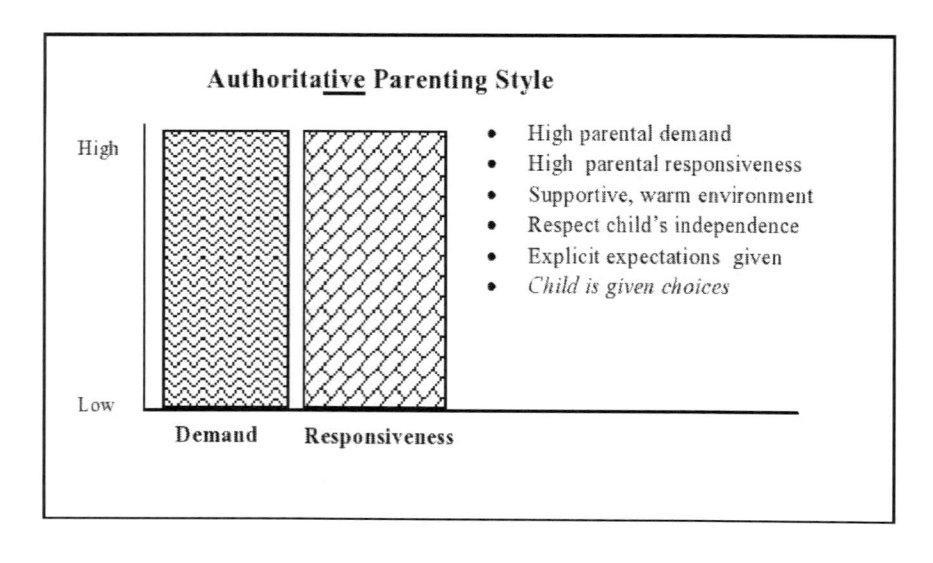

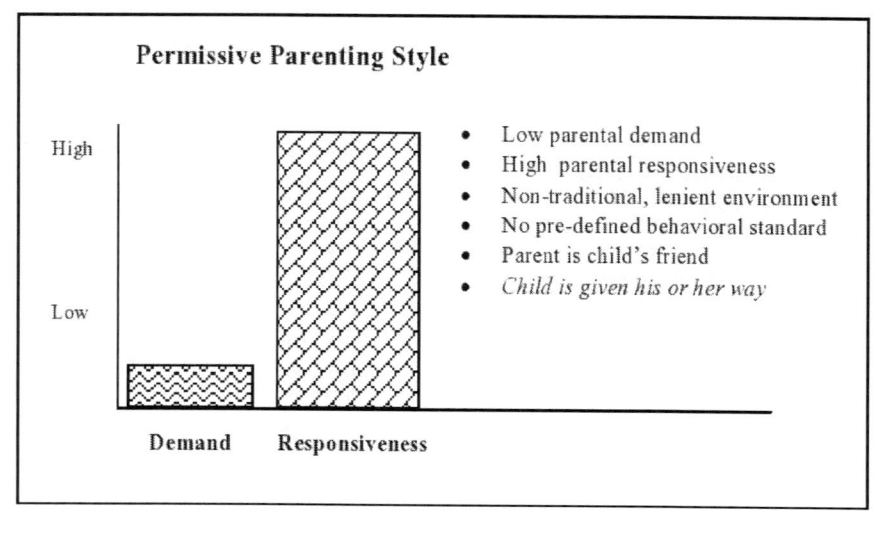

- Low parental demand
- High parental responsiveness
- Non-traditional, lenient environment
- No pre-defined behavioral standard
- Parent is child's friend
- *Child is given his or her way*

It is worth noting here that Dr. Baumrind's observational studies gave rise to parenting styles, not to teaching styles. At some after her studies were published in the mid 1960's, a bait-and-switch occurred. Dr. Baumrind's parenting styles magically transformed into classroom teaching styles. Why was this transformation a problem? It was and is a problem because there was never any objective evidence that home, familial parenting styles and public, institutional teaching styles have anything to do with each other. Proponents of Dr. Baumrind's parenting styles extol the superiority of the Authoritative style over the rigid Authoritarian and the lenient Permissive styles. Yes, several clinical studies do prove that children reared in Authoritative homes get higher grades than children from Authoritarian and Permissive homes. But this is where the objective evidence ends. There has been no education-based research that does not start with Dr. Baumrind's familial parenting styles as a presupposition for classroom based hypotheses. In other words, the precious few classroom management comparison studies that have been done all start with the presumption that Dr. Baumrind's home parenting styles are undeniably valid in the public classroom setting. This is a travesty for American education.

For the past few decades American schools have used the Authoritative teaching model at all grade levels. This teaching style is easy to recognize. A teacher stands in front of the class and puts out information for the students to learn. After several weeks, the student is expected to take an exam on the information the teacher taught. American teachers receive special training on providing supportive, warm environments while giving the student some degree of choice and encouraging student independence. But it does not matter how much we praise the Authoritative teaching model, the harsh reality is that American students continue to sink in the international academic ranks.

Authoritative teaching is not the answer to our educational woes. To save our school from falling further behind, we must stop acting like no catastrophe is going on and take a fundamentally different approach to student learning. Across cultures, civilizations and eras, the brightest minds throughout human history tell us that the best way to learn is simply to teach. In the 19th century, American education reformer, John Dewey and the

Hungarian-born mathematician, George Polya made the clearest arguments about the superiority of the learn-by-teach method over all other learning methods.

John Dewey's Learn-by-teach Method

Born in Burlington, Vermont to a family of modest means, John Dewey (1859-1952) became one of America's brightest philosophers, psychologists and education reformers. No, John Dewey did not come up with the Dewey Decimal System. That distinction belongs to Melvil Dewey, also an accomplished educator, but 8 years John's senior. These two Deweys were not related to each other. John graduated from the University of Vermont, taught high school for a couple of years, then enrolled in John's Hopkins University where he earned his Ph.D. In 1894 he became a professor at the University of Chicago. It was here that Dewey published several influential articles on education for which he became known as the Father of Progressive Education. So influential were Dewey's writings to the fields of Philosophy, Psychology and Education, that the United States Postal Service celebrated his life by putting his name and picture on a U.S. stamp in the "Prominent Americans" series.

John Dewey was ahead of his time. After spending a few years teaching high school he saw how futile passive learning was. He embarked on a vigorous campaign against the traditional education model which placed teachers at the front of classrooms as oracles of knowledge, teaching from pre-fabricated curricula. He wrote that "the purpose of education should not revolve around the acquisition of a pre-determined set of skills, but rather the realization of one's full potential and the ability to use those skills for the greater good" (Dewey, 1938). Dewey believed that students must be allowed to experience and interact with the curriculum in a real, practical way. He was careful not to minimize the teacher's importance in the education experience. He did not believe that students should completely control the curricula. He maintained that the teacher's role was still essential, but as facilitators or enlightened guides, helping students become lifelong discoverers by actively engaging the material instead of passively absorbing it.

Another 19th century education reformer was George Polya. Polya was born in Budapest, Hungary on December 13, 1887. He attended elementary school and high school in Budapest. In high school, he studied several languages, including Greek, Latin, German and Hungarian. He excelled in both biological sciences and in literature, but only earned satisfactory marks in math. His average performance in math was apparently due to poor teaching. Later in life, when Polya reminisced about his high school teachers, he described several of them as "despicable teachers" (O'Connor, 2002). He went on to attend both the University of Budapest and the University of Vienna where he fell in love with math. After graduating from college he was appointed to the math teaching staff at the Swiss Federal Institute in Zurich. Polya received two Rockefeller Fellowships that allowed him to study with mathematical geniuses in Oxford and Cambridge, England. Later when he was given an opportunity to complete a third fellowship at Princeton University in New Jersey, Polya took an immediate liking to the US. Several years later when political unrest forced him out of Zurich, he immigrated to the US. After teaching math at Brown University and Smith College, he joined the math teaching staff at Stanford University and made significant contributions to problem solving methods in higher math.

Polya was particularly skilled at cultivating within students the ability to solve complex math problems, specifically proofs. A mathematical proof is a convincing (logical) written demonstration that a math statement is true, or makes sense. Teaching proofs to university-level math majors is an art in and of itself. Polya was quite masterful at it. He had a special approach to teaching proofs --- put the student in the driver's seat and allow him or her to feel the emotional ups and downs that come with working their way through the proof. Polya's approach was so successful that he took the same approach to problem solving in general. He wrote that,

> The experience of problem-solving, with its selective attention and emotional charge, is part of the educational purpose: Your problem may be modest; but if it challenges your curiosity and brings into play your inventive faculties, and if you solve it by your own means, you may experience the tension and enjoy the triumph of discovery. Such experiences at a susceptible age may create a taste for mental work and leave their imprint on the mind and character for a lifetime (Larvor, 2010).

Polya understood that the most important skill that any teacher could cultivate within students is the ability to stand on their own two feet and solve problems using their unique compliment of intuition, memories, intelligence and drive. When discussing the ultimate objective of teachers, he said that "the aim is to reproduce in the student the problem-solving skills and mental habits of the teacher" (Larvor, 2010).

Although Dewey and Polya took very different paths to academic prominence, both of them ended up making the same discovery --- in order to learn, students must teach. Unfortunately, Dewey and Polya's conclusion was not adopted by U.S. schools. Contemporary school boards still task their teachers with presenting information from pre-fabricated curricula within very short periods of time. Students do not have the time to genuinely process the material or integrate it into their core selves. They only have time to memorize the material for short periods of time so that they can recognize it on multiple choice exams. Students repeat this pattern each week for months, semesters and years. From the 6th grade until high school graduation is only 12 semesters. After high school graduation we release our youngsters into the world thinking that the practice of short-term memorizing followed by post-exam dumping constitutes an education. Some of them go on to college and continue this "pump & dump" pattern because to them, that is what "getting an education" means. I have actually met adults with Bachelor degrees in Biology who had never heard of pheromones nor the Central Dogma of Molecular Biology. But, they could show me their carefully framed, decorative diploma hanging prominently on the wall.

But a few American schools are getting the iTeachMe message and are abandoning the authoritative, pump-and-dump instructional model. In January 2011, the National Urban Alliance sponsored a teacher training workshop in Newark New Jersey where students and teachers switched roles. Students actually taught the teachers while the teachers picked up clues for how to make their own teaching more relevant to the student's interests. This *student as teacher* exercise was conceived by the National Urban Alliance trainers when they observed "how easily students on the playground seemed to teach one another the latest dances or games" (Hu, 2011). Referring to the children's ability to teach each other dances or games on the playground, the group's chief of staff, Ahmes Askia said, "It's just so natural for them, their friends get it, and they get it almost effortlessly, so we're saying to the teachers: use that in the classroom" (Hu, 2011).

The only shortcoming with the NUA's teacher training program is that it did not go far enough, or should I say, long enough. The *student as teacher* part of the program is just that --- a part of a teacher training program. When the teacher training program was completed, the teachers returned to the traditional authoritative teaching model. The value of the *student as teacher* activity was that the student engaged the material in a fundamentally different way than they did when they were sitting in their seats in absorption mode. During the training activity the students became active learners, much like those students became at St. Johns University, one of the only universities in the US with a permanent *student as teacher* curriculum. Few people would know better that student as teachers become active learners better than St. John University Professor Jody Skinner.

Skinner studied philosophy and comparative literature at several universities in the US before moving to Germany as an exchange student. He ended up staying in Germany where he earned PhDs in German Linguistics and English Literature. Professor Skinner helped implement Germany's nationwide student as teacher curricula and facilitated the program for 15 years when he asked,

> What's the best way to motivate listless, uninterested students? Simply turn them into teachers! The technique practiced at several schools and universities, most notably at St. John's College in Annapolis, Maryland, and at more and more grammar schools in Germany is called Learning by Teaching and requires a radical shift in the traditional roles of teacher-learner. The results are overwhelmingly positive, especially in the field of foreign language instruction. Learning by teaching is not an exclusively modern didactic method. Seneca wrote 2000 years ago, docendo discimus: "We learn by teaching." At St. John's College, students teach each other philosophy and physics, ancient Greek and the integral calculus by using the "Great Books," the original works of Euclid, Shakespeare, Newton, and Freud (Skinner, 2009).

Skinner has known about the real benefits of student as teacher activities for decades now. Many of the teachers who participated in the in National Urban Alliance's teacher training workshops seem to be just now realizing or re-discovering these same benefits. "For Ms. O'Bryant, the [NUA] workshops have reinforced her belief that students can learn best when they are teaching one another. When she is the only one running lessons, she said, students sometimes tune out or do not pick up the material, no matter how many times she repeats it" (Hu, 2011). It would be a sad state of affairs if the NUA's *student as teacher* model does not supplant the traditional authoritative model in every high school, Junior college and University from sea to shining sea. After all, it happened in Germany over three decades ago.

Germany Adopts Learn-by-teaching as a National Model

Professor Jean-Pol Martin was born in 1943 in Paris, France and immigrated to Germany in 1968. In order to become a teacher at a German grammar school, he had to learn how to speak German as fluently as he did French. In 1980 he became a professor of foreign language in Bavaria. Professor Martin quickly observed that German students mastered the French language much faster when they taught their French lessons to each other. Martin was bold. He immediately ran an experiment in his classroom, much like the National Urban Alliance's *student as teacher* where all of his students took turns teaching each other. The experiment was wildly successful. He called his new method *Lernen durch Lehren*. The spelling may look a little strange because it appears here in German and literally means, *learning by teaching*. The *Lernen durch Lehren* method is usually written as the acronyms, LdL. This re-discovered technique is not simple tutoring; it is a process where students maximize their comprehension of concepts by teaching the concepts to their peers under the watchful guidance of professors. With the support of Germany's Federal Ministry of Education and Research, Professor Martin and his colleagues (including Professor Jody Skinner) began implementing the LdL method throughout all of Germany.

Lernen durch Lehren is now a fixture in Germany's education system. It has been well studied and validated a teaching method quite superior to the authoritative teaching model. Since 1985 more than one hundred doctoral students wrote their theses on the LdL method. By 1987 Martin and his colleagues had managed to establish an extensive LdL network consisting of several thousand teachers. Currently, all teachers in Germany are now trained to incorporate LdL into their curricula. Germany has consistently out ranked the United States in Reading, Science and Math (Organization for Economic Co-operation & Development OCED). Not only does Germany continue to improve its own education system with the LdL method, but has exported the method to both Japan (Oebel, 2005) and Russia (Rachimova, 2007).

What Must We Do to Save Our Schools From Sinking?

The federal and state governments must stop enforcing the same old failed education policies like the No Child Left Behind (NCLB) Act. The federal NCLB law uses meaningless, state-defined standardized tests to categorize schools as bad or good. Good schools get money and bad ones get sanctions, which is just pressure to appear like a good school. But like we discussed before, even the students from our good schools do not perform well when compared to their age-matched international students. Of course, the bad schools perform even worse, but they must now endure the added burden of sanctions. School boards from those states and districts with bad schools have figured out how to "dumb down" their standardized tests to make it seem like their students are performing well. Some school districts don't even put forth the effort to dumb down their standardized tests. They simply change students' answers from wrong ones to correct ones before submitting the exams to higher authorities. Whichever method these schools use to feign academic achievement, their motivation is to avoid sanctions and receive more federal dollars. The NCLB Law therefore incentivizes schools across the country to create only an illusion of academic excellence. There is no elusive, undiscovered system of standardized testing that can improve the U.S. education system. This law undermines any genuine effort for administrators to actually improve student comprehension or to help them take an education.

Teachers must stop teaching the same old pre-fabricated curricula, giving hints about which information will be on the test. Parents must turn off Reality TV, set up a home study environment and provide and audience so that their high school students can teach their homework. Students must begin maximizing their comprehension by teaching their homework assignments at home each night to anyone who will listen. Old Testament Jewish parents were commanded to teach their children the Mosaic Law in the morning, noon and night. Undoubtedly, the parents internalized the Law because they were required to teach it so frequently. We can use the same principles here with students. When doing homework, students should not sit at home and input, input, input. They should input at school, and briefly at home, if necessary. But the bulk of their homework time should be teaching homework assignments to their parents or whoever else will listen. If no real audience is available, then the students should teach an imaginary audience, a pet, a pillow or a chair --- whoever or whatever they choose to teach, it is an absolute must that they teach.

Both John Dewey and George Polya would have been thrilled to hear about NUA's teacher training program and that it has spread to schools in San Francisco, Connecticut, Indiana, Georgia and New York. It is my hope that the NUA's training program represents a glorious move away from the traditional authoritative teaching model to a student-centered learn-by-teaching model. Although this transition will be a difficult one for teachers, it can be done. Daniel Lu, a special education teacher who participated in the NUA teacher training program said that "as a teacher, it's really hard to give up control of your classroom. I think we have to trust our students more to work together" (Hu, 2011). Mr. Lu's sentiment could very well be the prevailing sentiment of authoritative teachers all across the United States. But the only way to reverse our county's academic decline is to make students teach. Herein lies hope for American education. The international community had better not count us out. We know how to save our schools. Our Titanic just might not sink after all.

Chapter 4
The Sacred Self

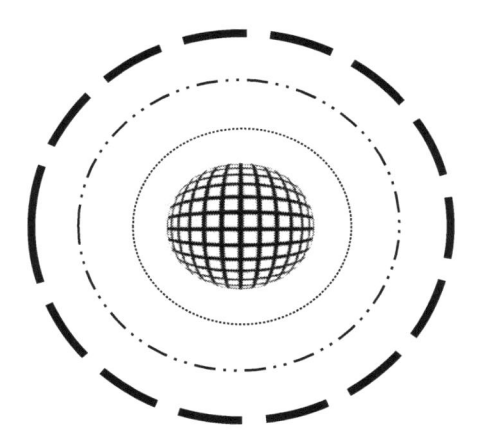

So, we know the difference between getting a diploma and taking an education. We also understand that the circumstances of a person's life cannot prevent them from taking an education. We saw how Dr. Neil Flemings' widely accepted VARK learning styles grossly underestimates our mind-brain's dynamic ability to learn. In the last chapter, we were encouraged to exchange blind exceptionalism for an evidence-based view of our education system. This evidenced-based view not only revealed that American education is sinking but that our intellectualism is too. We were urged not to sit idly by and let this insidious catastrophe unfold. Most importantly, we discussed the single most important, proactive intervention that would save our schools --- the iTeachMe home study method. The brightest minds in human history continually re-discover that learning-by-teaching is the best method for stimulating the creativity required for a society's continued technological development. But what is so special about America's iTeachMe or Germany's LdL methods? How can they produce a generation of intellectuals while the current authoritative teaching model produces anti-intellectualism? The answer is --- long-term memory. In this chapter I want to delve a little deeper into the organization of the mind-brain and how this organization makes iTeachMe and LdL the absolute best methods for maximizing student comprehension.

The mind-brain is mysterious. I suspect that it is much more advanced than contemporary science realizes. The mind-brain has the ability to operate on many levels and in many dimensions all at the same time. When information is learned, it is stored in either the short-term or in the long-term memory bank. The individual chooses which bank is used. As a general rule, we remember what we intend to remember. Students who sit in class absorbing knowledge from the teacher for the purpose of regurgitating this same knowledge on a future exam will store that knowledge up until the exam. After the exam, they may see little use for retaining the knowledge and dump it into the sea of forgetfulness. Traditional authoritative teaching models have produced this type of pump-and-dump cycle commonly seen at all grade levels.

Our mind-brains do not experience the world through linear VARK modalities. Just think about how you experience the world around you. Time may be linear, but your mind-brain certainly is not. Your mind-brain functions more like concentric spheres, where each smaller sphere is a deeper level of consciousness. The innermost sphere is very essence of you; it is sacred; it is what you would call *self*. Look at the diagram below. Self is fully immersed in, surrounded by and connected to long-term memory. The long-term memory is abutted by the working (or short-term) memory, which is abutted by the ultra-short-term (or Sensory Memory), which is constantly bombarded by environmental stimuli. The interaction between your innermost sphere (self) and your innermost space (long-term memory) is your limbic system. We will discuss the three types of memory in a little more detail later. For now, just understand that each sphere is encapsulated by a porous barrier, a filter of sorts. This system of filters is called the reticular activating system or RAS for short.

Figure 4.1
Environmental Stimuli and Mind-Brain Interface

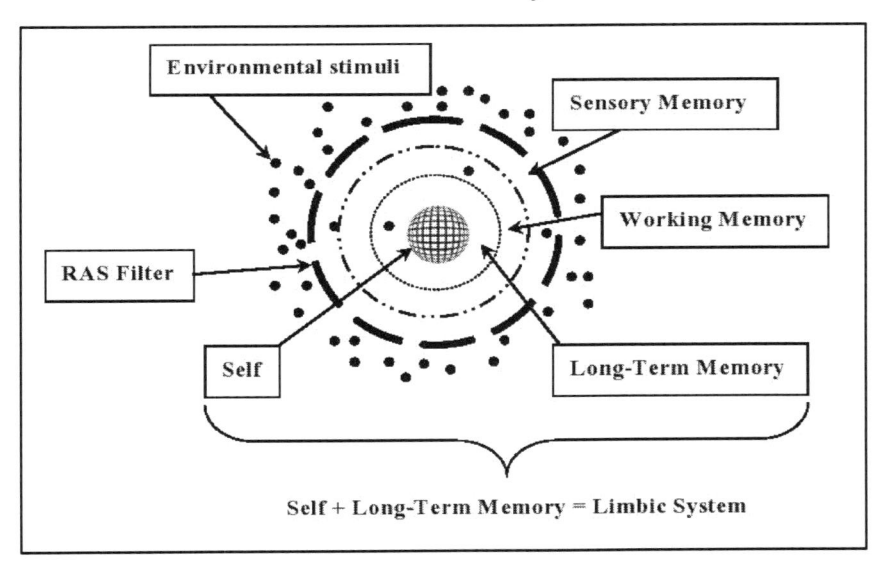

This mind-brain model is not mumbo jumbo. The RAS is a system of nerve connections that originate in the upper brainstem and project to the thalamus (sensory integration center) and to the higher brain centers (the cerebral cortex). The RAS controls a person's wakefulness, sleep mechanisms and functions as a multilayered system of preferential filters. Yes, the term *preferential filter* seems redundant. After all, aren't all filters by definition preferential, allowing some substances to pass through while blocking others? This is true. But the added function of the RAS is that it instantly alerts the person when any preferred (or important) stimulus actually gets through. Not just any old filter can do that.

Figure 4.2
Outflow Tracts of the Reticular Activating System (RAS)

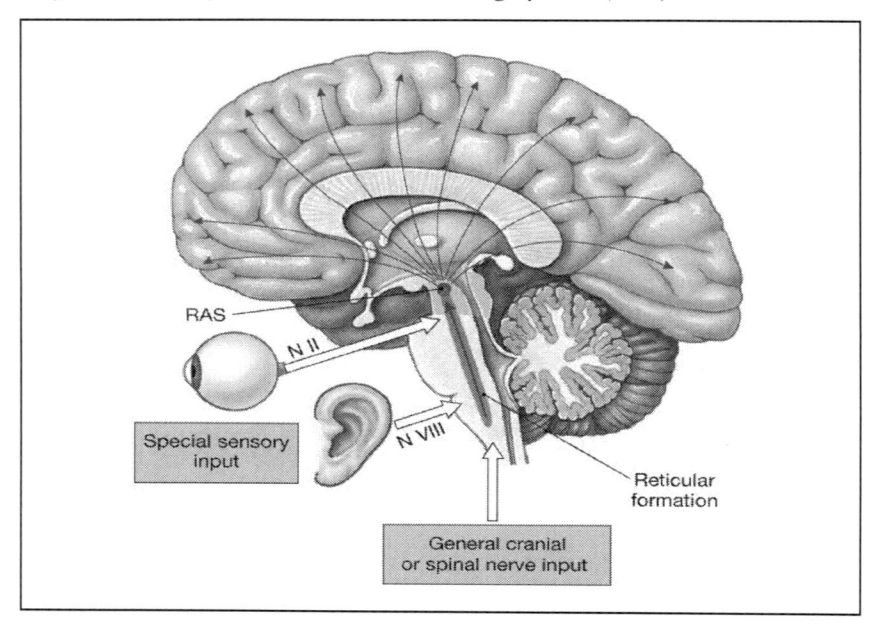

For example, say you are riding on a noisy subway train, teeming with commuters having a thousand conversations, shuffling newspapers, clearing their throats, so on and so forth. All of this sensory information is reaching your brain simultaneously. Your RAS filters out all of this meaningless information. You do not notice the sounds of the train, the babies crying, the tantrum of an insolent toddler, the pressure that the hard seat exerts against your buttocks, the texture of your watchband against your wrist, or the conversation of the passenger seated next to you. But if someone, anyone calls your name or if the conductor announces your particular destination stop, then your RAS instantly alerts your conscious mind to pay attention to that particular information.

So, what criteria does your RAS use when *deciding* which information to suppress and which information to let through to your conscious mind? There is only one criterion --- personally identifying meaningfulness. Basically, the only information that is allowed to reach your deliberate consciousness is that which has meaning, *as determined by you*. The sound of your name is deeply meaningful to you. The name of your subway destination stop is meaningful to you. Notice the *"to you"* part. Before you pay attention to any sensory information in your environment, the information must first bombard your outermost sphere and also be considered meaningful to you. The mother sitting across the aisle from you can say "sit down now" and you would ignore her. But that mother's distinctive voice would catch the attention of her little insolent brat careening up and down the middle aisle. So, meaningfulness is a relative term. On the subway, each stimulus filtered out by your RAS is meaningful to someone else on the train --- just not to you.

Not only is meaningfulness necessary for extraneous information to get through your RAS filter into your conscious mind, but it is also necessary for important information to enter your long-term memory from your short-term memory. When important information, like, a math formula, an amino acid structure, or details from the French-Indian war need to be remembered for more than a few weeks, such information must first be found meaningful. Making information meaningful is the most efficient way to store it deep within the core of ourselves.

Accessing the Sacred Self

The *sacred self* and the *innermost core* are just other ways to refer to a person's heart. Proverbs 4:23 says "Guard your heart above all else, for it determines the course of your life" (NLT). This sacred scripture suggests the enormous power of our hearts to determine everything else about us. Empty hearts mean empty lives. So, if we want our children to grow up to live full, meaningful lives, we must put the right kinds of stuff inside their hearts. If we want a nation of informed, reasonable-minded adults, we must instill within our children a thirst for knowledge, research and critical thinking.

And just who should be charged with instilling these values in our children? Well, us! That's who. By us, I mean our entire country. Whenever any country needs to meet some collective need, that country establishes a social institution. A social institution is not some large, sprawling building with a well-manicured lawn. A social institution is all of the collective activities within society aimed at meeting a specific need. For example, Americans have a specific need to send and receive packages. So, what rises out of all of our business and government activities is a package delivery institution. This institution includes the US Postal Service, United Parcel Service, FedEx, DHS, transportation vehicles, delivery insurance, etc. Social institutions always reflect the shared values of the dominant group within that society.

To meet the collective need of educating our country's youth, we established the institution of compulsory education. No parent can forego having their child educated. Parents are required by law to enroll their child in some type of school, whether it is a public, home, or charter school. Although our country has decided to educate our young, our educational system does not exist to produce scholars or thinkers. It currently exists to instill social and religious values into our youth, insuring that future generations share the current generations' values and remain good citizens. But herein lays the problem. While a reasonable person's definition of a *good citizen* is someone who loves the country and follows its laws, not many segments of our population share this *reasonable person* perspective. Depending on the region of the country you're in, local communities and school boards frequently attach specific social and religious behavior requirements to their definition of good citizens.

Many school boards do not actually want students to think for themselves. When students think, they eventually begin to challenge the values dearly held by the adult school board members and community leaders. It is like Helen Keller said, "people don't like to think. If one thinks, one must reach conclusions. Conclusions are not always pleasant" (Loewen, 2007). This is why American History books adopted by school boards invariably delete any negative aspect of actual American history and present only a whitewashed, cartoon-like, feel-good perspective. School boards supply these textbooks and the curricula to go with them. They place authority figures, or teachers, in the classroom to indoctrinate students. Teachers who do not present the approved curricula are sanctioned or simply removed. Some of our school boards are busy enacting school policies prohibiting the word "gay" from being uttered on school grounds. Many of our school boards are engaged in an epic battle to have religious doctrines like the creation story included in science curricula. Is there any wonder why American students continue to fall further behind other nations in critical thinking, math and science? Look what our school boards try to instill in them. As a nation, we must stop trying to instilling non-academic concepts into our children in the school setting. It is already difficult enough for teachers to access the students' deeper consciousness levels. It is already difficult to get students to commit important concepts to their long-term memories. The rare occasions in which teachers manage to reach these deeper spheres (i.e. their hearts), all too often non-academic information is being deposited. Plainly put, moral and religious values should not be instilled at school, but at home or in places of worship.

We know that every student has spheres of consciousness in which they hold memories for varying lengths of time. Before teachers can change their teaching method to get access to these deeper spheres, teachers must decide what should be deposited. Teachers can choose to deposit information or process. I think the choice is obvious. Here, the old adage applies. Give people a fish and you'll feed them for a day. But teach them how to fish and you'll feed them forever. So, given the choice between information and process, teachers should instill process. Instead of forcing students to memorize a list of mathematical formulas by rote, teach the student how to derive each formula from real world experiences.

Of course, this approach may frighten establishment teachers, who are very comfortable using the authoritative "teacher knows best" model. In their argument against making any change, they may extol the sanctity of instilling information rather than instilling process. They may claim that time is too limited to teach anything other than packets of information. To them, information is critical. Curricula must be followed; all else be damned! But I beg to differ. Most of the time, information is not that critical. Let's look again at how American History is currently taught. Remember how high school textbooks present a whitewashed, cartoon-like, feel-good view of American History. Any reasonable person who has lived into their 30's would immediately recognize that this textbook view of American History does not show the real nature of people. W.E.B DuBois said it best,

> One is astonished in the study of [American] history at the recurrence of the idea that evil must be forgotten, distorted, skimmed over. We must not remember that Daniel Webster got drunk but only remember that he was a splendid constitutional lawyer. We must forget that George Washington was a slave owner --- and simply remember the things we regard as creditable and inspiring. The difficulty, of course, with this philosophy is that history loses its value as an incentive and example; it paints perfect men and noble nations, but it does not tell the truth (DuBois, 1935).

Eighty-three percent of Americans do not take another history course after high school (Loewen, 2007). These Americans become the vast majority of our citizenry who earnestly believe that the fairytales they heard during high school history is the actual history of our country. Yes, this distorted perception of our true history contributes to our blind exceptionalism and intellectual decline, but this perspective does not immediately destroy us. So, at least for American History, the quality or accuracy of the information is not critical.

Instilling process is better than instilling information. Remember what George Polya said about the duty of teachers --- to create within the student the mental habits of the teacher (Larvor, 2010). The choice between teaching information versus teaching process is the choice between nurturing Neanderthals and creating creators. But how do teachers even get access to their students' deeper spheres? The answer, make them teach. How do teachers teach process over information? The answer, make them first attach meaning to the information that they teach. There are even better questions: how do students access their own deeper spheres? How do they learn process as opposed to many bits of information? The answer, apply the iTeachMe method at home. How do students learn process? Whenever the teacher presents new information, the student should ask the "whys," then teach the "whys" at home using iTeachMe. Notice the paradigm shift here. No longer should students sit quietly in their seats while the all-knowing teacher lectures at the front of the class. At home, the student should rarely sit quietly and re-read, highlight or underline the text book. These are passive modes of learning. Knowledge and concepts are not likely to pass from the short-term memory to the long-term memory from highlighting a textbook. Using the iTeachMe method will help students become active learners, first at home, then at school. This is how students can learn the mental habits of their teachers and begin educating the core of themselves --- their sacred selves.

Benefits of Active Learning

So, the iTeachMe method helps students access their sacred selves but also requires them to become active learners. Classroom-based research shows that the vast majority of college and graduate school students are passive learners. One particular study conducted on 20 different college campuses surveyed 566 students and 20 professors concluded that "learning appeared to be a spectator sport" (Nunn, 1996). This same study showed that only 6% of college class time is actually spent on student participation. Numerous studies, confirm the common sense notion that students demonstrate better retention the more they participate in classroom discussions. This positive correlation between participation and concept retention is not just true at the college level. High quality participation-performance studies done with elementary and junior high school students show this same positive correlation

(Wolfgang, 1973). These findings are good news for students with Attention Deficit & Hyperactivity Disorder (ADHD). According to the American Academy of Child and Adolescent Psychiatry, ADHD is a common behavioral disorder affecting approximately 8% to 10% of school-age children. Boys are affected three times more than girls. Children with ADHD tend to act before thinking, are hyperactive and find it difficult to stay on task.

> Some children with ADHD continue to have it as adults. Quite often adults who have the disorder are not even aware of it. They may feel that it is impossible to get organized, stick to a job, or remember and keep appointments. Adults with ADHD are challenged by basic daily tasks such as getting up on time or preparing to leave the house for work. They also tend to struggle with failure at school, problems on the job and even failed relationships. Like teens, adults with ADHD may seem restless and may try to do several things at once, most of them unsuccessfully. They also tend to prefer short cuts rather than taking the steps needed to achieve greater rewards (NIMH, 2009).

Both children and adults with ADHD tend to learn more efficiently when they are physically active. Dr. Fleming would label them as kinesthetic learners. He may be correct, but like I mentioned before, a kinesthetic learner can also use other learning modalities. Perhaps school-aged children, with higher metabolic rates and less social inhibition than adults simply have a greater need than adults to get up and move around. Remember the National Urban Alliance teacher training workshop where the students were made to teach? "The half-dozen students who participated told their teachers that they learned better when they could get up, move around and interact with their classmates." (Hu, 2011).

Moving large muscle groups on a regular basis improves brain function. Even senior citizens who become physically active after being sedentary for long periods of time experience nerve cell regeneration in their hippocampi (Y.E. Geda, 2010). It has long since been known that the brain gets the most blood flow and has the most widespread global activity when a person is standing up (Ouchi, 1999). This is the reason why humans cannot sleep standing up. The simple act of standing up requires global activation of the brain, with a large number of neurons firing off to maintain the right balance of muscular contraction and relaxation. Standing is an exceedingly complicated process for the mammalian brain. I am not even talking about moving around while standing; I'm just talking about standing still in one spot. Standing in one spot involves complex interactions between the autonomic nervous system, which regulates blood pressure, and cerebral auto-regulation, which maintains adequate blood flow to the brain (Olufsen, 2005). But aren't horses mammals too? Why can horses sleep standing up? The short answer is --- they can't. Horses and cows only appear to sleep standing up because they have four legs which can be locked out to hold their body weight, much like fold-out legs to a portable table. This brain-leg joint coordination is called the "stay apparatus" and is only active during non-REM (rapid eye movement), swallow sleep also known as dozing. Horses and cows can only doze while standing up. They cannot sleep standing up. During deep sleep too many regions in the brain, including the "stay apparatus" become dormant. Even horses and cows must lie down to get deep sleep.

Why all of this talk about physical activity, brain cell regeneration in the hippocampus, and brain activation during standing? Because knowing the structure and function of the brain allows us to better design leaning mechanisms to better utilize the brain's natural learning abilities. We can better learn how to ---

well, learn. For example, when we understand that the brain gets more blood flow when a person is standing up moving around, then maybe our schools will stop punishing ADHD children for exhibiting what the teacher recognizes as hyperactivity. After all, school aged children have been very clear about telling education researchers that they learn best when standing up, moving around. Neuro-anatomical research supports these children's' claims that upright, active learning is probably more efficient learning. Unfortunately, American schools cannot let go of the traditional authoritative teaching model where the dictator teacher demands that the students stay quietly perched in their seats, giving their undivided attention. I say hog-wash! This is why the iTeachMe method does not allow students to learn while sitting or lying down. iTeachMe students learn while standing up, walking around teaching their homework. This is also the reason why the iTeachMe method is particularly beneficial to teens and adults with ADHD. As you will see in the next chapter, iTeachMe students do not teach when they are sleepy or tired. When a person feels sleepy, their brain is saying "I require rest; I need to rejuvenate." During these times the mind-brain does not efficiently transfer new information from the short-term to the long-term memory (Alhola, 2007). Tired students cannot attach meaning to knowledge.

Human Memory

When we talk about accessing the sacred self and how body position and sleep affect cognitive ability, it is useful to also talk about how our memory actually works. Remember that the human mind-brain does not simply learn by seeing, hearing, reading or doing. It learns by doing all of these things plus more, and all at the same time. If the mind-brain needs to store any concept long-term, that concept must first be deemed meaningful by the individual. So when the student successfully stores new information in his or her long-term memory (core self or heart), this new concept has traversed the student's outer spheres of consciousness. Indeed, the concept has traveled through the RAS filter, into the sensory memory space, then into the short-term memory and finally into the long-term memory.

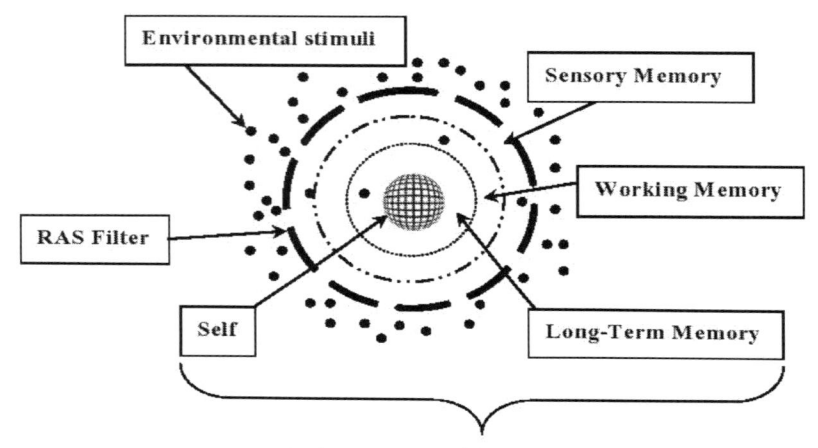

Self + Long-Term Memory = Limbic System

We can place all human memories into one of three categories: sensory, short- term and long-term. Because there is no need to maintain a mental record of every bit of sensory stimuli that we have ever encountered, our mind-brain selects which stimuli to remember and for what length of time. This mental retention of sensory information is called memory, specifically the sensory memory. All memories begin with perception. A congenitally blind person could never remember what Mount Rushmore looked like. He never received the initial visual impression of the monument onto his visual cortex. Of course, sensory perception is just the beginning of memory formation. But much of what we perceive is simply not meaningful to us; we have no use for it. So this trivial sensory information is quickly forgotten, lasting in our consciousness for mere fractions of a second. This sensory information is trivial, but not useless. It is this type of information that allows us to recognize patterns, sounds, smells or tastes.

Imagine you are driving fast on a congested freeway. Your exit is coming up and you are in the middle lane. You need to move over into the right lane to make your exit. You turn on your signal light and quickly glance over your shoulder to see if that lane is open. Now, you do not have to keep looking over your right shoulder for the entire duration of this traffic maneuver. You quickly get a visual perception of the available space; then you change lanes. You intuitively perform distance and speed calculations, not only for your car but for the other cars immediately around you. You probably do not recognize that you are performing simultaneous distance and speed calculations, but you are. Now let's fast-forward 60 minutes. So, you have managed to safely change lanes and make your exit. You are now at home preparing dinner. You do not remember the details of how much space was available between your car and the trailing care when you were trying to change lanes only an hour ago. You do not remember if the brake lights were activated on the car that was in front of you. Such information was useful only for that brief moment when it was needed. It is not meaningful to you now; your mind-brain has no need to store such information in the deeper spheres of your consciousness.

The next, deeper level of memory is the short-term memory. The short-term memory is also called the primary or active memory. You have read where I refer to a person's deliberate consciousness. This is also the short-term memory. The short-term memory can store small bits of information for short periods of time. These "short periods of time" vary widely from person to person but typically ranges from a few seconds (when no rehearsal is performed) to several weeks (when rehearsal is performed). By "rehearsal" I mean the act of repeating the information over and over again until it can be readily recalled. The short-term memory can store about five to nine pieces of information before the purging (or forgetting) process begins.

Another type of memory that is similar to short-term memory is the working memory. The working memory "refers to a brain system that provides temporary storage and manipulation of the information necessary for such complex cognitive tasks as language comprehension, learning, and reasoning" (Baddely, 1992). Many people use a combination of their short-term and working memories to manage their day-to-day affairs, remember routes, plan out their week, or recognize shapes and spatial relationships of things in their environment. Many students use their working memory to recognize the correct answers on multiple choice exams. The neurons responsible for short-term and working memory storage are located in the pre-frontal cortex, just behind the forehead. Sensory information can be made to cross into the short-term or the working memory by rote memorization techniques. But just like the sensory memory bank has a limited storage capacity, short-term and working memory banks have limited storage capacities as well. There are some instances when a person can use rote memorization techniques to move information from the short-term or working memory deeper into the sacred long-term memory. A person would be interested in doing this because the long-term memory has virtually unlimited storage capacity. This is why I describe the long-term memory as sacred. What you put there stays there.

Long-term memory refers to the continuing and permanent storage of information. Information that reaches the sacred long-term memory resides largely outside of the person's deliberate consciousness. But this is not a problem because this information is most readily summoned or called back into the working memory to be used when needed. Recall from chapter two that the long-term memory is physically and functionally connected to the limbic system. While the short-term memory can only store five to nine bits of information at once, the sacred long-term memory naturally stores hundreds of thousands of facts, details, experiences, facial expressions, linguistic expressions, idioms, likes and dislikes that have been accumulated over a person's lifetime. Albert Einstein's theory of Relativity was not stored in his short-term memory; it was stored in his sacred long-term memory.

So we have learned here that in order to educate the deep core of ourselves, we must do more than just memorize concepts for mere regurgitation or recognition on multiple choice exams. We must allow scholarly information to traverse our external memory spheres to reach our deeper consciousness levels. Just because a particular concept is vitally important does not mean that it will easily pass from our external environment into our long-term memories. For any concept, important or not, the price of admission into our hearts is genuine understanding. What better way to learn the first law of Thermodynamics in physics than to genuinely understand how energy, work and heat relate to each other in the real world? A physics teacher can either help students discover these relationships themselves or make the students sit quietly in their seats and recite this law over and over again. The first method produces the likes of Albert Einstein; the second method produces poorly educated masses. The United States is at a crossroad. We can continue to down the road to mindless Reality TV connoisseurs, defining ourselves by the material things we own. Or we can lead the world into the 21st century by becoming a nation of scholars and innovators.

Chapter 5
How to do iTeachMe

The problem that many students have in school is remembering all of the information presented during daily lectures. For example, when my math instructor gives a lecture, he presents a new concept, works out practice problems on the chalkboard then assigns homework. The next class period is a repeat of the same process. This sounds appropriate enough. However, this teaching method does little to ensure that students have mastered concepts from previous lectures before having to grapple with newer concepts in subsequent lectures. In my math class we typically march through several weeks of lectures before an examination. Those students who did not master the concepts in the weeks before the exam typically get low test scores. Many of the students who do perform well on exams may forget much of what they learned soon after the test. This post-exam knowledge dumping seems to be more prevalent in the humanities, like literature, language, history and government.

Why does this post-exam knowledge dumping happen? It happens because many students initially learn the material with the intent of remembering it specifically for an upcoming exam. They do not master the material for the purpose of educating the core of themselves. Throughout human civilization, successive generations have been more advanced than the previous ones, the latter having the benefit of learning from the former. But compulsory education in America seems to be regressing with each successive generation. For students locked into a system that dispenses knowledge for test-passing purposes, trying to educate their hearts is a near impossible task. Many teachers have given up on their sacred mission of guiding students toward genuine educations. For example, throughout the country there are many elementary school math teachers who no longer require their students to show their work. Those students who turn in math homework as a list of answers may not have the slightest clue as to how the answer was arrived at. This is the 21st century; there are plenty of ways students can find the answers to math problems. Just a few minutes on the internet will do the trick. The defeated math teacher is not interested in understanding how his or her students arrive at their answers. The defeated History teacher does not require students to understand the root causes of the Civil War. These teachers are content to give the students a list of dates and battlefield names to commit to memory for subsequent recognition on multiple choice exams. Such teachers rob students of the opportunity to analyze the prevailing attitudes, mores and values in the United States during the seventeenth through the nineteenth centuries.

Students follow teachers. When teachers teach to the test, students focus their study activities on simply preparing to pass tests. Studying for the purpose of passing a test is a completely different experience than studying for the purpose of educating one's heart. The former focuses on repetitive inputting of information until the exam date. The latter focuses on the repetitive output of new concepts that the student has recently found meaningful. Repetitive input of meaningless information allows the student to regurgitate the same information back up on exams. Because the information had no real meaning to the student, they quickly forget most of it after the exam. But the repetitive output of meaningful concepts results in the life-long understanding of those concepts.

Step-By-Step iTeachMe Instructions

iTeachMe is a repetitive output study method to help you engage academic subject matter and to transfer newly learned concepts from your short-term memory into your long-term memory. In order to apply the iTeachMe method, you must learn four simple steps:

1. <u>Rapid Input</u> – Get new concepts in promptly.

2. <u>Cognitive Integration</u> – Weave the new concepts into a framework of existing knowledge.

3. <u>Active Output</u> – Teach the newly integrated concepts to another person or thing.

4. <u>Recursive Review</u> – Teach the new concepts over again until all knowledge gaps are filled.

Step 1: **RAPID INPUT**

Let's start with Rapid Input. Rapid input has everything to do with promptness and nothing to do with frantic behavior. It starts with you pre-viewing the subject matter that your professor will be presenting in class. This is very easy to do. Use your syllabus to find out what your professor is likely to teach. If your professor will be lecturing on chapter two in your textbook, before the lecture, read chapter two. As of this very moment, if you ever find yourself siting in class listening to a lecture that you have not previewed, then consider yourself behind the knowledge power curve for that day.

When your professors present new concepts during lectures, they rarely bombard you with a large number of them. They usually present a few new concepts within the confines of a broader theme. For example, in General Chemistry, the concept of the Heisenberg uncertainty principle that says that *the position and velocity of a particle cannot be simultaneously measured with a high degree of accuracy* is typically presented at the beginning of the school term under the broader theme of sub-atomic particles. Your Chemistry professor may spend only 10 to 15 minutes explaining the Heisenberg uncertainty principle and spend the remaining 30 to 40 minutes talking about 2 or 3 other concepts in the chapter. So, during the class period, only a few concepts are actually presented. Furthermore, many professors take a few minutes before their current lecture to review old concepts. They may also take a few minutes after their current lecture to take questions or have an open discussion. So, there is precious little time available to present even the few new ideas that are actually presented. At any rate, the first iTeachMe step, rapid input begins here, before each lecture.

Since several new concepts are presented in short periods of time, you must remain purposefully alert, ready to capture the salient features of each new concept presented. You can capture the salient features of newly presented concepts by taking careful notes or by using a digital tape recorder to record the lecture. Remember that rapid input begins before the lecture. But it is during the lecture that something critical happens --- the transfer of knowledge. During lectures you absolutely must pay attention. Of course, you should not skip lectures. Do not be late to class or sit in the back of the classroom. Do not be the class clown. As your professor presents the information, desperately try to understand the big picture first. If you feel confused during lecture, raise your hand and ask for clarification. You will be teaching this same material at home. So make sure that you genuinely understand it at the time it is given to you.

Whenever you receive any new concept during lecture, review your lecture notes and or listen to that particular lecture again before going to sleep that night. That's it. You have completed rapid input. Notice that rapid input has nothing to do with frantic behavior or rapid-fire activities. It has more to do with being proactive and getting information from the textbook or from the lecture promptly into your head.

Step 2: **COGNITIVE INTEGRATION**

Step 2 of the iTeachMe method is cognitive integration. During cognitive integration you will be weaving the information that you learned during rapid input into knowledge that you already have. Look at cognitive integration as your effort to connect the new information to something in your life that you can easily remember. For example, if you are studying General Chemistry and you are learning about how electrons behave in an atomic orbital, you are likely to learn about Hund's Rule. Hund's Rule says: *Every orbital in a sub shell is singly occupied with one electron before any one orbital is doubly occupied, and that all electrons in a singly occupied orbital must have the same spin*. So, how would you integrate this principle into your existing knowledge or attach it to some previous experience. Well, first you must look in your textbook or ask your professor to explain any word within Hund's Rule that you do not understand. You should not try to integrate Hund's Rule into your existing knowledge base without knowing what the terms *electron*, *atomic orbital* or *electron spin* mean.

This information is very easy to get. So once you understand that an electron is some magical-sounding thing that acts both like a particle and a wave, something more aptly called a *warvicle*, and that they spin like spinning tops, and that an orbital is one of many little rooms arranged around a central, positively-charged proton then you are ready to integrate. You also read in your textbook that electrons (or warvicles) have a negative charge. Then you think of the beautiful Paula Abdul and her pop song, *Opposites Attract* and immediately remember from playing with magnets as a child that similar magnetic poles repel each other. So you figure that warvicles are attracted to protons while simultaneously being repelled by each other. Cognitive integration is going on here.

As you continue to integrate, you know that warvicles are spinning negative charges that can only live inside of little rooms (orbitals) arranged around a central proton. Ah ha! You then recall a past experience of yours that involved you riding in an elevator (which is a small room that humans temporarily occupy for transportation). You recall that whenever several strangers get into an elevator they generally maximize the distance between each other. This behavior is near automatic. You also remember that the same stranger-distance pattern holds for any situation that calls for strangers to occupy close quarters, like loading up a bus. Before two strangers share the same seat, they will automatically distribute themselves into one person per seat before doubling up. There you have it. You have successfully integrated Hund's Rule into your unique, life experience. Now Hund's Rule does not seem that complicated at all. You now understand that because two warvicles have the same negative charge, they will repel each other. And like strangers loading up a bus, warvicles will not doubly-occupy the same orbital (or seat) until all orbitals (or seats) are singly occupied. This is cognitive integration.

Cognitive integration may take you longer than it takes others, depending on the subject matter, your age, life experience and other factors. But remember that no matter how difficult the concept may seem at first, you have the ability to define the terms used to describe the concept then find some existing knowledge or past experience to attach the new concept to. This cognitive integration step is especially important for iTeachMe because the next step, active output --- during which you teach the new concept to a real or imaginary audience --- cannot be done unless you have performed cognitive integration first. You cannot teach what you do not understand. Do not try to skip this step.

The main reason why you must never skip cognitive integration is that integrated knowledge is the only type of knowledge that becomes meaningful to you. Meaningless knowledge must always be forgotten. This is why you simply do not remember random facts devoid of meaning. For example, let's say that your U.S. History professor is teaching you about our Civil War. He teaches that many battlefields have two names, one given by Confederate soldiers and the other given by Union soldiers. To prepare you for an upcoming exam, your professor tells you to learn the two names of the battlefield on which the bloodiest battle of the entire war was fought --- Sharpsburg and Antietam. Of course, you are a responsible student and commit the battlefield names to memory. After all, you care about passing the test. But six months after the test you (or others students in your class) may not be able to recall the battlefield names. But what if your professor, instead of teaching you random facts, like battlefield names, taught you about the underlying causes of the Civil War? Whichever side you would identify with, the North or the South, your own passions would likely begin to stir in your heart. You probably would be more interested in learning that the Confederate Army was more dependent on support from local townsfolk than the Union Army. You would more likely commit to memory that the Confederate Army named battlefields according to the closest town while the Union Army named the same battlefields according to the nearest body of water. I am willing to bet that 50 years from now you will still remember that Antietam is a river near the Maryland town of Sharpsburg. Do you see what happens when you add meaning to random facts? The information easily gets stored into your long-term memory.

Step 3: **ACTIVE OUTPUT**

The most recognizable iTeachMe step is active output. The iTeachMe logo is a little red, round-headed person teaching behind a lectern. The little red person is doing active output. Active output is the act of teaching newly-integrated concepts to a real or imagined audience. During this step get the chance to explain old concepts in new terms --- your terms. Yes, you can apply your personal life experience and world view to historical or traditional knowledge. This is how successive generations discover new scientific truths and advance technologically. Students who are trapped in traditional authoritative schools where all-knowing teachers transplant old knowledge into young minds are not likely to become innovators or creators. They are not likely to push the limits of scientific discovery. Another benefit of the active output step is that you give yourself the opportunity to check how well you understand particular concepts. Put another way, when you do active output, you can discover gaps in your understanding. These gaps are called knowledge gaps. Knowledge gaps should be discovered at home days before you sit for an exam. You should not discover them during an exam when you are <u>required</u> to demonstrate mastery of the material. If you have knowledge gaps during your exam you will receive low grade. But even if you do not have knowledge gaps you can still get low test scores. You may have test anxiety or not feel comfortable putting out information under the pressure of a timed exam. This is one of the many reasons why you must practice active output daily at home and not occasionally at school, during exams.

Active output requires you to teach newly integrated concepts in an organized, structured manner. This structured manner prepares your mind to store the material logically in your long-term memory. Before you perform active output, prepare your study environment. Make sure you have the necessary equipment. Do not make excuses for why you cannot prepare your study environment. Do not attempt to perform active output in a noisy room, with the TV on, when you are sleepy or when you do not have the required 60 minutes. These are the items and the environment necessary for doing active output:

1. A well-lit, quiet room
2. One 48" x 37" iTeachMe Dry-Erase Wall Chart
3. A waist-high table (preferably the Adjustable iTeachMe Two-Tiered Lectern, supplied by the iTeachMe Company at www.iteachme.net)
4. Your textbook or classroom notes (for the subject that you will be teaching)
5. A pack of 3x5 index cards with an ink pen
6. Dry-Erase Markers and an eraser. (It is preferable to use the "Click-it" dry-erase markers supplied by the iTeachMe Company. The writing tips on these markers can be retracted into the body. Retracting the tips will prevent them from drying out too frequently during the teaching hour.)

Now that you have all of the necessary items and have found a quiet, well-lit room, this is how you set up your teaching environment:

1. Affix the iTeachMe Dry-Erase wall chart to the wall with 12 Command® Strips provided with the chart. Make sure that you have plenty of space on the floor in front of the wall chart to pace back and forth as you teach. Three to four feet is pacing space is adequate.

2. Position the Adjustable iTeachMe Two-Tiered lectern 3-4 feet in front of the wall chart, facing away from the wall chart. During active output, stand behind the lectern with your back to the wall chart.

3. Place your textbook and / or classroom notes, along with your dry-erase markers and eraser on the top tier of the lectern. Place your 3x5 index cards and ink pen on the bottom tier of the lectern.

Now that you have prepared your teaching environment, it is time to start teaching. To get the most out of the iTeachMe method, you should only teach or perform active output in 60-minute time periods before taking a break. Use the first 5 minutes to write a simple outline for what you will be teaching. Then spend the next 45 minutes teaching and identifying your knowledge gaps. Then spend the final 10 minutes presenting a summary of what you just taught. What follows is a sample treatment of a topic with the time-activity breakdown of what you should be doing during the active output step:

Outline: (5 Minutes)

Spend no more than 5 minutes writing a standard Roman numeral outline of the subject matter to be taught during this teaching hour. For example, if the subject matter is "Modes of 20th Century Transportation," then the outline should be written in the "Outline Area" on iTeachMe dry-erase wall chart like this:

> ### MODES OF 20TH CENTURY TRANSPORTATION
>
> I. Non-motorized Land Vehicles
>   a. Horse-drawn Carriages
>   b. Human-drawn Carriages
>   i. Human-drawn Carriages in the Orient
>   ii. Human-drawn Carriages in the West
> II. Non-motorized Water Vehicles
>   a. Row Boats
>   b. Sail Boats
>   c. Model-T Ford

<u>Teaching</u>: (45 Minutes)

For the next 45 minutes, you should teach the subject matter using your outline as a guide. You can occasionally glance at your textbook or classroom notes sitting on the top tier of your lectern. It is vitally important that you not read from the textbook or classroom notes. As a matter of fact, the only time you should even touch your textbook or classroom notes is to turn the page. For most of the 45 minutes, you should be standing behind the lectern, much like a Rabbi, preacher or priest stand behind a podium. You should turn around frequently to write, draw and diagram the concepts that you are explaining on the iTeachMe wall chart. Draw and write in the middle part of the wall chart labeled, "Teaching Area." While you may choose to mimic your school teacher's teaching style, you should try to develop your own style. Use your imagination as much as possible when you teach. If you can imagine it, draw it. Albert Einstein wrote that "imagination is more important than knowledge. While knowledge defines all that we currently know and understand, imagination points to all we might yet discover and create." Now, this is extremely important. When you are teaching, proceeding down your outline, as you come across particularly important concepts or terms, stop teaching briefly and write the name of that concept or the term on the right side of your wall chart in the "Key Term" area.

You will not be able to teach every subject smoothly. Sometimes you will not remember what your professor or what your textbook says about one topic or another. Do not worry about this. Whenever you get to a part of your outline that you don't know well enough to teach --- hurray! You just discovered a knowledge gap that you can fill before your exam. Don't squander this opportunity. Get a 3x5 index card that should be sitting on the lower tier of your lectern and <u>immediately</u> write down exactly what seems unclear to you. Do not be formal here. Be unapologetically you. For example, if you are teaching according to your outline on twentieth-century modes of transportation and you get to an unfamiliar part about the types of diesel locomotives, you could write on your 3x5 card: *I haven't the slightest clue how a diesel-hydraulic locomotive is different from a diesel-mechanical locomotive.* Because these 3x5 cards are notes to yourself about your knowledge gaps, these notes are called "gap notes." Immediately after your teaching hour ends, sit down with your textbook or classroom lecture notes and fill in your knowledge gaps.

<u>Summary</u>: (10 Minutes)

After teaching for 45 minutes, you should take an entire 10 minutes to present a summary of your lecture. Erase the middle portion of your wall lecture chart and use the outline and the key terms to navigate through your summary.

Step 4: **RECURSIVE REVIEW**

The 4th iTeachMe step is recursive review. No one can discount the importance of regular review to promote the long-term retention of meaningful concepts. In iTeachMe, this review takes place at least three times over seven days, at 24, 48 and 72 hours after your initial teaching hour. To keep track of the lessons that you teach, you should write down the textbook section heading or other identifying name of the subject matter that you teach in your Recursive Review Planner that comes with the iTeachMe wall chart. Keep this planner in the same vicinity of your wall lecture chart. The best option is to hang the review planner on the wall next to your wall lecture chart. The review planner hangs open like a wall calendar so that you can conveniently keep track of your lecture topics. Try to teach each topic or chapter section four times (one hour each) before you sit for an exam on that material. This is how the iTeachMe recursive review schedule looks like:

Figure 5
Recursive Review Schedule

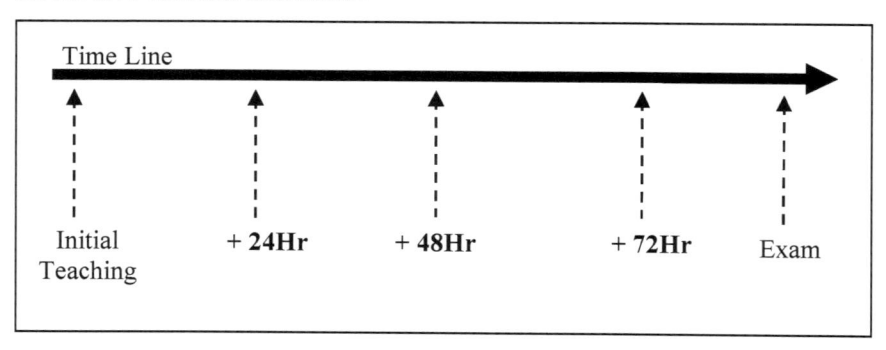

```
Time Line ──────────────────────────────►
    ▲         ▲         ▲         ▲         ▲
    ┊         ┊         ┊         ┊         ┊
 Initial    +24Hr     +48Hr     +72Hr      Exam
Teaching
```

This type of review is described as "recursive" to emphasize the importance your teaching the same, exact lecture at least four times before an exam. You will know that the information is reaching your long-term memory by the decreasing number of gap notes that you make with successive teachings. Once again, it is important that you see gap notes as opportunities to fill in the gaps in your knowledge before you sit for any exam. This self-analysis activity is called Continuous Comprehension Analysis (CCA) and is what sets the iTeachMe method apart from other study methods. This is how you can guarantee yourself straight A's throughout your academic career.

Final Thoughts on iTeachMe

So, there you have it. The four iTeachMe steps are Rapid Input, Cognitive Integration, Active Output and Recursive Review. Just as with learning any new process, learning the iTeachMe method will feel awkward at first. You may be tempted to modify these steps or cut corners. This would be a mistake. The iTeachMe method compliments the natural way that the human mind-brain learns. You should start off by teaching only a few new concepts during a teaching hour, being careful to follow the steps described above, without deviation. It is important that you use the iTeachMe method in your current classes so that you can see how much better your comprehension and test scores will be. This is the best way to build confidence in the new study method. Of course, the more you use the iTeachMe method, the better you will become at it. Soon, in the matter a few weeks, you will begin to see the many academic and intellectual benefits of the iTeachMe method.

In this book, you have learned that regardless of life circumstance, many people can educate their hearts. We discussed the mind-brain's dynamic ability to learn, despite the popularity of the VARK learning styles that underestimate the mind-brain's ability to learn on different levels and in different dimensions simultaneously. We briefly surveyed Gestalt psychology and saw how Gestaltism better explains how our mind-brain learns. We investigated the mechanisms of human memory and differentiated among sensory, short-term and long-term memory. We now know that for new concepts, the price of admission into the long-term memory is meaningfulness. After considering how the mind-brain learns and remembers, we presented the iTeachMe home study method, not new method, but merely a re-packaging of an earlier, ancient one by which the brightest humans educated their hearts, hearts that still shape the course of human civilization.

Appendix A

iTeachMe Preparation

To perform the iTeachMe method successfully you must prepare yourself and your environment for one hour of uninterrupted time. While it is more beneficial for you to do the iTeachMe method in front of an audience, you must be prepared to perform the study method without anyone else present. This is how you set up your teaching environment:

1. You will need to hang the iTeachMe lecture chart on the wall in a well-lit room. Use the Command™ strips to hang your wall chart with the center of the chart at the level of your eyes. Make sure that you have enough uncluttered space to pace back and forth in front of the wall chart.

2. Set up a table in front of the wall chart, approximately 3-4 feet away from the wall. The table should come to the level of your belly button. It is highly recommended that you use the iTeachMe Two-Tiered Lectern available for purchase on the iTeachMe Company's website.

3. Place your classroom lecture notes or your textbook on the top tier and place twenty 3x5 index cards and a writing pen on the lower tier. If you choose not to use the iTeachMe Lectern, then just place your textbook, classroom notes and 3x5 cards on whichever table you have available.

4. Place your dry-erase markers and eraser on the top tier (or table). Now you are ready to go.

Appendix B

iTeachMe Steps (60 Minute Sessions)

1. Outline the Lesson: **(5 minutes)**
   Spend the first 5 minutes writing the outline of what you will be teaching for the next 45 minutes. Write the outline in standard Roman numeral format on the "Outline Area" on your wall chart.

2. Teach the Lesson: **(45 minutes)**
   Stand in between your wall chart and the lectern, with your back toward the wall chart most of the time. Spend the next 45 minutes teaching according to your outline. Do not skip around; be disciplined and stick to your outline. Write and draw pictures and diagrams on your wall chart in the "Teaching Area" as you teach. When you teach a key term or a key concept, write the term or concept on your wall chart in the "Key Term" area. It is important that you teach from your own understanding of the concepts that you recently learned during the Rapid Input and Cognitive Integration iTeachMe steps. Do not read from your textbook or classroom notes. You may glance briefly at your textbook or classroom notes to guide you to the next concept. You should only touch your textbook or classroom notes to flip the page.

   Create Gap Notes: **(Perform while teaching)**
   During your 45 minute teaching time, you will come to an outline subject heading that you are unable to explain well. This represents a gap in your knowledge. This is a good thing. You

have the opportunity to make a note of this knowledge gap BEFORE you take an exam on this subject matter. Record your knowledge gap by writing on a 3x5 index card the specific concept that you were unable to explain. These cards called "Gap Notes."

3. <u>Summarize the Lesson</u>: **(10 minutes)**
   After you have taught for 45 minutes, stop teaching and spend the next 10 minutes summarizing what you just taught. Use your outline and your key terms to guide you through your summary.

4. <u>Continuous Comprehension Analysis</u>: **(Time varies)**
   Immediately after ending your 10 minute summary, sit down and relax with your newly created gap notes. Use your textbook and or classroom notes to read over those areas that you were unable to explain during your teaching session. Make sure that you have filled the gaps in your knowledge before getting up.

Appendix C

Germany's Lernen Durch Lehren
(Learning By Teaching)

The Goal:
The overall objective of *Lernen Durch Lehren* (LdL) is to prepare high school and university students for communication in knowledge societies.

The Core Idea:
The core idea is to have a student or a group of students instruct a topic to their classmates, but: in a way that activates the classmates' participation and communication in the best possible way.

It is not the student experts' task to just present an issue in a structured way, but to think about ways that have their classmates find the solutions for questions and thus only gradually reach a structured knowledge at the end. This way learners are also given the chance of acquiring creativity, independence, self-confidence and key competences, such as the ability to work in teams, the ability to communicate, complex thinking, the competence to seek and find information, explorative behavior, presentation skills, project competence, internet skills, structuring information and generating knowledge; punctuality, reliability, patience. The role of the teacher is one of preselecting or suggesting topics, of giving guidelines to the student experts regarding didactic possibilities and the relevance of contents, of assisting student experts during preparation and in class, of observing the learning process reflected by the actions and reactions in class, and of guaranteeing that, despite potential problems, every learner will know at the end what the main insights or conclusions of the lesson were supposed to be. Teacher and students are conceived as partners, the hierarchy is flat.

Academic Basis:
Research on information and (developing) knowledge societies has shown that members of such societies need the following three pillars of competences:

1. A broad general knowledge
2. Various pieces of expert knowledge acquired through the realization of own projects
3. A catalog of
   a) Personal competences, e.g.
      - Maintaining self-discipline
      - Resisting mental fuzziness
   b) Social competences, e.g.
      - Communicating empathically in an atmosphere of trust, openness, cooperation, efficiency
      - Working well in a team
   c) Methodological competences, e.g.
      - Carrying out a project (setting a question/goal, finding the right method) (project competence)
      - Finding and evaluating information in various sources, especially internet competence
      - Presenting a project and its result in the internet
      - Transferring information into applicable knowledge
      - Translating expert knowledge into generally intelligible language with a focus on communication between human and human, not between human and machine

Studies from learning psychology, biology and education show that the following ingredients are vital for effective learning:

- Possibility for self-fulfillment (sense in life, "world improvement competence")
- Affective attachment toward contents
- The experience of flow effects
- An active exposure to the contents ("grasping" their meaning)
- The presentation of contents in a familiar "language" (in a familiar register)
- The presentation of contents through intelligible metaphors and analogies

- Autonomy in content selection, recurrent scrutinizing of knowledge
- Learning in a community

Father of LdL:
Jean-Pol Martin, professor for teaching and key competences, teacher trainer

A "Son" of the Model:
Joachim Grzega, associate professor for linguistics, teacher trainer

Appendix D

Author Biography

Ever since his days at Bakersfield Junior College, in Bakersfield, California, Dingane Baruti has enjoyed tutoring math and the sciences. As a tutor, he was vigorously sought after. He based his tutoring style on Dr. Michael L. Jones' book, *The Overnight Student: How I Went From Straight F's to Straight A's.* Baruti was not always so keen on education or academic pursuits. He was born, Patrick Donahue Dean in Bakersfield, California on August 26, 1971 to a fundamentalist Christian, working-class family. The 5th of five boys and a little sister to follow, Dean spent four of seven days in church for the majority of his childhood. He took well to reading, cover to cover, a Children's Bible that his mother, Mary Ann Dean bought him for his ninth birthday. His favorite part of the bible was the Book of Judges, which told the story of Samson, Delilah and the Philistines. He learned that story and other biblical stories so well, that at age 11 he was invited by the pastor of his church to teach these stories to other young people in Youth service.

By the time he was 13, Dean was teaching these stories and preaching by invitation in other churches and at conventions throughout California. To better understand the bible, he became engrossed in analyzing the hermeneutics and biblical history books in his father's study. Dean was not the typical teenager; he thoroughly enjoyed researching biblical patterns and typology, the 12 Apocryphal books, translation and linguistic variances among the John Wycliffe, William Tyndale and the King James versions of the bible. His intense interest in biblical study was only matched by his lack of interest in secular education. He spent practically no time studying math, science or any other secular subjects. At Bakersfield High School, he earned mostly D's, a few C's and a few F's. His poor academic performance was ignored by both his parents and the high school faculty. But Dean kept up his religious studies and speaking engagements. Although his school grades were horribly low, they were just high enough for his continued progression from the 9th through the 12th grades.

By the time he was 17 Dean's life was characterized by ironies. He was quite the biblical scholar, committing the entire Book of Hebrews to memory and would routinely quote entire chapters from memory. But he remained uninterested in secular academics and cared very little about his 1.8 G.P.A at Bakersfield High School. He was regarded as a preacher of sorts but was not successful in suppressing his physical desires for his first serious girlfriend. He and her began a sexual relationship and immediately became pregnant. Because of this, Dean stopped preaching and teaching and moved out of his parent's home. He got a part-time job at Bakersfield Machine Company, sweeping metal shavings off the floor. He focused on meeting the bare minimum graduation requirements. While his girlfriend was pregnant, Dean received a high school diploma, despite never having taken Algebra. When asked about his not taking Algebra in high school, Dean reports the he was quite amazed at the people who could do math using letters instead of numbers.

Just before he turned 18, Dean's life was in shambles. The Bible was only thing that he confidently knew. He lived with whichever family member could spare a couch or living room floor. He was a soon-to-be teen dad with no education or marketable skill. Black teenage males in similar predicaments typically ended up hustling on the street, in prison, dead or, at best, languishing in some menial job for 40 years. But Dean took another unlikely path --- the military. While riding with his girlfriend's sister, he looked up and saw a billboard with an expertly-dressed U.S. Marine under the caption, "Uncle Sam Wants You."

The next day, Dean caught the city bus to the recruiting office. The Marine recruiter was out to lunch but the Army recruiter's door was wide open. Dean enlisted in the Army as field medic. He completed basic training at Ft. Knox, Kentucky and his field medic training at Ft. Sam Houston, Texas. While he was in Texas, his daughter Lakai Monee Banks-Dean was born. After he completed his field medic training at Ft. Sam Houston, Dean took leave for 2 weeks to see his daughter. He was then sent to Camp Pelham, South Korea for a 1 year tour. Camp Pelham was on the far north end of South Korea, only several miles South of the Demilitarized Zone between North and South Korea. At Camp Pelham, Dean worked closely with medical doctors who had attended medical school in Bethesda, Maryland at the Uniformed Services University of the Health Sciences (USUHS).

Dean saw how these doctors used scientific knowledge to relieve physical suffering. He was hooked. There, in South Korea at age 18, he decided to become a medical doctor. He immediately enrolled in a basic math course, taught by a local Korean instructor who could barely speak English. This is where Dean learned basic math. Excited that his one-year tour of duty in Korea was coming to an end, Dean was crushed when the Joint Chief of Staff of the Army, General Colon Powell froze all Army permanent change of station (PCS) moves. The date was January 15, 1991; the United Nations had just declared war on Iraq who had invaded Kuwait, 4 months earlier. Operation Desert Shield had officially turned into Operation Desert Storm. It would be another year before Dean would leave South Korea and return to the United States.

When he did return, he only had nine more months left on his enlistment contract. He spent those nine months working as a medic on the Vascular Surgery ward at Walter Reed Army Medical Center in Washington D.C. While in Washington D.C., Dean visited the medical school that he had heard about back in Korea, more than a year ago. He resolved within his heart that, not only to become a physician, but that he would specifically attend USUHS for medical school.

After completing his last 9 months of active duty, he moved back to Bakersfield, CA to start junior college. During his admissions counselor meeting, Dean told the counselor that he wanted to be a physician. The counselor reviewed Dean's high school transcripts and his 1.8 GPA and advised the bright-eyed prospective student to set a more realistic career goal, recommending several certificate programs and trade schools. Upset by the counselor's recommendation, Dean told the counselor that she should feed his fire, not try to quench it. He rejected her recommendations and went to see a different counselor the next day. With the new counselor, Dean started the conversation by saying, "I am only interested in becoming a physician; please show me how to get there." After reviewing Dean's high school transcripts and dismal GPA, the counselor explained the placement testing and basic prep courses that would be required.

Dean spent the next two years taking the most basic Math, English and Science classes that Bakersfield College had to offer. He worked the graveyard shift at Wal-Mart full-time while taking 12 to 18 units each semester. After two years of remedial classes, Dean then spent another two years taking Zoology, Botany, General and Analytic Chemistry and Physics. He took every Math class that the college had to offer, up to Integral Calculus. After a total of four years at a Junior College, Dean transferred to the University of California at Davis, majoring in Biochemistry. After two years of rigorous study, he graduated with a Bachelor of Science Degree in 1998. A year before he graduated from U.C. Davis, Dean had already applied USUHS for medical school. At 8:35 AM on November 27, Thanksgiving Day 1997, Dean received a phone call from USUHS informing him that he had been accepted into the next year's class.

Dean frequently describes his four years of medical school as the best four years of his life. He reports being in awe of the intricacies and the sophistication of the human body, from each individual cell all the way up to complex interaction of people within large populations. Dean never regarded scientific truth as the antithesis of God, but a mere expression of his handiworks. Dean graduated from medical school in May 2002 and started his Family Medicine Residency at Martin Army Community Hospital, Ft. Benning, GA. During his residency, Dean's mentors made a tremendous and lasting impression on him. Together, mentors such as Dr. Clark Cobb; Dr. Patrick Contino; Dr. Mark Higdon; Dr. Sharon Maxwell; Dr. John O'Brien; Dr. Karen O'Brien taught Dean that the secret to caring for patients is to actually care about them. These mentors also taught Dean to always maintain the heart of an inquisitive, thinking physician despite the ever-increasing pressure from Capitalistic Medicine to erode the physician's ability to provide thoughtful, compassionate care. They taught him that Family Medicine is a specialty concerned with identifying the abnormal among countless permutations of normal. Dean learned that a person is not their disease. He learned to approach every patient by considering the complex interaction of their personal habits, family history, cultural dispositions and motivations.

This approach to patients led Dean to evaluate his own life, his family history and cultural dispositions. As a result of a deeper insight into himself, his family and the African American culture, Dean legally changed his name from Patrick Donahue Dean to Dingane Baruti. Asked why he changed his name, Baruti responded "as I continue to learn more about myself and my background, I have determined that my name should reflect my character and my family's character. My first name should say something about who I am while my last name should acknowledge my ancestors. Although Baruti acknowledges that his ancestors were most likely brought to the United States from West Africa, he found a most fitting South African, first and last name. *Dingane* means one who searches; *Baruti* means teacher. After Dr. Baruti completed his Family Medicine Residency, he served as a Battalion Surgeon in Iraq (2005-06). After returning from Iraq, he joined the Family Medicine Department at Bayne-Jones Army Community Hospital at Ft. Polk, Louisiana until 2008. In the summer of 2008, he moved back to Ft. Benning, GA and currently provides expert medical care to the greatest Soldiers in the world.

Bibliography

Anissimov, M. (2011, February 09). *What is the Limbic System?* Retrieved May 17, 2011, from Wisegeek: www.wisegeek.com/what-is-the-limbic-system.htm

Carroll, Y. (2002). *A Hymn for Eternity: The Story of Wallace Hartley, Titanic Bandmaster.* Gloucestershire: NPI Media Group.

Chronicle Research Services. (2010). *The College of 2020: Students (Executive Summary).* North Hollywood: The Chronicle of Higher Education.

Cournot, M. e. (2006, October 10). Relation between body mass index and cognitive function in healthy middle-aged men and women. *Neurology* Vol 67. No. 7 , pp. 1208-1214.

Dewey, J. (1938). *Experience and Education.* New York. MacMillan.

W.E.B. DuBois. (1935) *Black Reconstruction* (p. 722). Cleveland: World Meridian.

Gross, C. G. (2000, October). Nature Review: Neuroscience Volume I. *Neurogenesis in the Adult Brain: Death of a Dogma* , pp. 67-73.

Harrison, B. C. (2008). *Power and Society.* Belmont: Wadsworth Publishing.

Hochschild, J. L. (2003, November). Social Class in Public Schools. *Journal of Social Issues.* Vol.59 (4):821-840

Hu, W. (2011, January 14). *Teacher Training; Taught by Students.* Retrieved May 22, 2011, from New York Times: Newark Journal:http://www.nuatc.org/articles/pdf/ny_times_2011_01_15.pdf

Kunjufu, J. (1982). *Countering the Conspiracy to Destroy Black Boys.* Chicago. African American Images.

Larvor, B. (2010). *Authoritarian vs authoritative teaching: Polya and Lakatos.* Retrieved May 21, 2011, from University of **Hertfordshire**: http://hdl.handle.net/2299/4479

Lee, J. M. (2010). *The College Completion Agenda 2010 Progress Report.* Reston, VA: The College Board (Report can be downloaded at http://www.completionagendea.collegeboard.org.).

Loewen, J. W. (2007). *Lies My Teacher Told Me.* New York: Touchstone.

MCEF. (2002). *Success for Every Student? Tracking and the Achievement Gap.* Montgomery: Montgomeray County Education Forum.

NCEE. (1983, April). *A Nation At Risk.* Retrieved April 22, 2011, from National Commission on Excellence in Education (Archived Information): http://www2.ed.gov/pubs/NatAtRisk/risk.html

NCES. (2005). *International Outcomes of Learning in Math, Literacy and Problem Solving.* Washington DC: National Center for Education Statistics.

NLT Bible. *New Living Translation.*

Nunn, C. E. (1996). Discussion in the College Classroom: Triangulating Observational and Survey Results. *The Journal of Higher Education. Vol. 67, No.3* , 243-266.

OCED. (n.d.). *Programme for International Student Assessment (PISA).* Retrieved March 17, 2011, from Organization for Economic Co-operation & Development (OCED): http://www.oecd.org/document/53/0,3343,en_32252351_32235731_38262901_1_1_1_1,00.html

O'Connor, J. (2002, November). *George Polya.* Retrieved May 20, 2011, from School of Math and Statistics; University of St. Andrews, Scotland: http://www-history.mcs.st-andrews.ac.uk/Biographies/Polya.html

Oebel, G. (2005). *Lernen durch Lehren (LdL) im DaF-Unterricht. Krisenbewältigung im Fach Deutsch als Fremdsprache in Japan.*

Page, W. T. (1918, April 3). *The American Creed.* Retrieved May 24, 2011, from Historic Documents: www.ushistory.org/documents/creed.htm

Rachimova, A. (2007). *Multimedia in der Ausbildung.*

Rohrbach, D. (2007, December). The Development of Knowledge Societies in 19 OECD Countries Between 1970 and 2002. *Social Science. Vol 46, Number 2* , pp. 655-689.

Skinner, J. (2009). *The Koblenz Model within Anglo-American Cultural Studies at German Universities.* Retrieved May 22, 2011, from Developing Teachers.com: http://www.developingteachers.com/articles_tchtraining/koblenz3_jody.htm

Spera, C. (2005, June). A Review of the Relationship Among Parenting Practices, Parenting Styles, and Adolescent School Achievement . *Educational Psychology Review. Volume 17, Number 2* , pp. 125-146.

US Census Bureau. (2009). *S1501. Educational Attainment.* Retrieved April 12, 2011, from US Census Bureau: American FactFinder: United States; 2005-2009 American Community Survey: http://factfinder.census.gov/servlet/STTable?_bm=y&-geo_id=01000US&-qr_name=ACS_2009_5YR_G00_S1501&-ds_name=ACS_2009_5YR_G00_&-redoLog=false

Wolfgang, A. e. (1973). *Internality as a Determinant of Degree of Classroom Participation and Acadmenic Performance Among Elementary Students.* Montreal, Canada: American Psychological Association: 81st Annual Convention.

Xu, R. (2007). *How Do Chinese Students Learn and Study?* Retrieved Feb 13, 2011, from Centre for Teaching, Learning and Assessment. The University of Edinburgh: http://www.tla.ed.ac.uk/interchange/summer2007/xu1.pdf

Made in the USA
Lexington, KY
18 November 2011